Attorneys General: Enforcing the Law

★★★ IN THE CABINET ★★★
Attorneys General: Enforcing the Law

Phyllis Raybin Emert

The Oliver Press, Inc.
Minneapolis

For Diane Stein . . . and, of course, Larry

Special thanks to Silvestra Puente Praino, Reference Librarian,
Mahwah Public Library, Mahwah, New Jersey

The Oliver Press, Inc.
Charlotte Square
5707 West 36th Street
Minneapolis, MN 55416-2510

Library of Congress Cataloging-in-Publication Data
Emert, Phyllis Raybin.
    Attorneys general: enforcing the law / Phyllis Raybin Emert.
       v. cm. — (In the cabinet ; 3)
    Includes bibliographical references and index.
    Contents: William Wirt: defining the office — Edward Bates: war, civil liberties, and
slavery — A. Mitchell Palmer: abusing the office — Francis Biddle: loyalty versus
conscience — Herbert Brownell: beginning the fight for equality — Robert F. Kennedy: the
struggle for civil rights — Edwin Meese III: politicizing the office — Janet Reno: first
female Attorney General.
    ISBN 1-881508-66-8 (lib. bdg.)
    1. Attorneys general—United States—Biography—Juvenile literature. 2. Justice,
Administration of—United States—Juvenile literature. 3. Law enforcement—United
States—Juvenile literature. [1. Attorneys general. 2. Justice, Administration of. 3. Cabinet
officers. 4. United States. Department of Justice. Office of the Attorney General.] I. Title.

KF372.E46 2004
349.73'092'2—dc22

                                                      2003064988

ISBN 1-881508-66-8
Printed in the United States of America
10 09 08 07 06 05   8 7 6 5 4 3 2 1

CONTENTS

★ ★ ★ ★

INTRODUCTION

The Evolution of the Attorney General

When Edmund Randolph became the first attorney general of the United States in 1789, he was frustrated by his small salary, his lack of power, and the fact that he had no office, clerk, or supplies. Being attorney general was not even a full-time job; in addition to serving his country, Randolph was expected to continue working as a lawyer in private practice. In a letter to a friend, he complained, "I am a sort of mongrel between the State and the U.S.; called an officer of some rank under the latter, and yet thrust out to get a livelihood in the former."

The position of attorney general, however, has expanded and evolved just as the United States has grown and developed over time. Today, the attorney general is the chief law-enforcement officer of the United States government and is the head of the Department of Justice (DOJ), a huge and complex institution. In 2003, the DOJ had a budget of $25 billion and employed about 120,000 people in 39 separate organizations. These included the Federal Bureau of Investigation (FBI), the Drug Enforcement Administration (DEA), the Bureau of Prisons, and the offices of U.S. attorneys and U.S. marshals throughout the nation.

The position of attorney general—a title borrowed from the British—was created in the United States by the Judiciary Act of 1789. It stated that a "person learned in

U.S. attorney: the lawyer in charge of prosecuting federal crimes within a certain judicial district of the United States, appointed by the president

The United States Department of Justice building in Washington, D.C.

7

The United States has two separate court systems, federal and state. In the federal system, the lowest courts are the district courts. (There are 94 judicial districts; some states have only one, while more populous states may contain several.) Above them, there are 13 circuit courts of appeals. There are also some specialized federal courts, such as the Court of International Trade. At the head of the federal system is the United States Supreme Court (which can also take cases from the state system).

cabinet: a group of presidential advisors that mainly consists of the heads of the executive departments of the federal government. Cabinet members are nominated by the president, but they must be confirmed by the Senate.

opinion: an attorney general's formal answer to a specific legal question asked by a public official; also, a judge's written statement announcing a court's decision and giving the reasons for it. An opinion by a court is legally binding, while an opinion by an attorney general is merely advisory, though it can carry weight in court.

the law . . . shall . . . prosecute and conduct all suits in the Supreme Court in which the United States shall be concerned, and . . . give his advice and opinion upon questions of law when required by the President . . . or when requested by the heads of any of the departments." The Founding Fathers wanted to establish a strong legal system to ensure the individual and political freedoms they fought for in the Revolutionary War. At the same time, however, Congress did not want to infringe on the rights of the states. Therefore, the specific duties of the attorney general were purposely left vague. The Judiciary Act created a federal court system and a national attorney general, but it did not directly link the two together. The attorney general would have no centralized authority over U.S. attorneys in the various states; he would supervise federal legal cases only when they reached the Supreme Court.

In the beginning, the job was a part-time position with low pay and few benefits. The attorney general earned a salary of only $1,500 per year in 1789, half what the secretaries of war, state, and treasury received. While these cabinet members headed departments with staffs and budgets, the attorney general worked alone and had to pay for any expenses out of his small salary. President George Washington had to convince his friend and personal attorney, Edmund Randolph of Virginia, to accept the position. Washington explained to Randolph that he could continue to practice law in addition to being attorney general. He also pointed out that the prestige of the office would help obtain clients for Randolph's private practice. Financial considerations were a high priority for Randolph, who was heavily in debt due to his years in public service and a number of bad real-estate transactions. Persuaded by Washington, Randolph accepted the job.

Randolph lived in Washington, D.C., only when the Supreme Court was in session. He researched and wrote his own opinions on legal matters, but kept no records of his work. The rest of the time he spent at home, attending

to his law practice, taking care of his ill wife, and revising the law code of the Virginia assembly. Yet during his four years as attorney general, Randolph set two important precedents that helped define the office for future administrations. First, although he did not head a department in the executive branch, Randolph began attending cabinet meetings regularly, beginning in March 1792. Since that time, all attorneys general have been regular members of the president's cabinet. Second, Randolph's close relationship with the president as both legal and policy adviser set a pattern that has continued to this day; presidents frequently appoint a friend as attorney general. Randolph became Washington's most trusted government ally, consulted for his opinion on political issues in addition to legal matters. He acted as a balance between opposing factions in the cabinet, often casting the tie-breaking vote between

"[R]andolph's] opinion always makes the majority; and . . . the President acquiesces always in the majority; consequently that the government is now solely directed by [Randolph]."
—Thomas Jefferson

rivals Secretary of State Thomas Jefferson and Secretary of the Treasury Alexander Hamilton.

Randolph also made three basic recommendations to President Washington regarding the role of his office. First, Randolph believed that the attorney general should be authorized to represent the government in lower courts, not just in the Supreme Court. Second, he thought the attorney general should be given centralized authority over lower-level U.S. attorneys nationwide. Third, Randolph recommended that the attorney general should be allowed to hire a clerk to record legal opinions. Washington submitted these recommendations to Congress, but no action was taken.

Little changed in the office of the attorney general for almost 30 years. It remained a part-time, low-paying cabinet position. The federal government was just another client who paid the attorney general for legal services. Finally, in 1819, Congress recognized the increasing responsibilities and legal workload of the job. It provided Attorney General William Wirt with a $3,500 salary; office space in the Treasury Department; an allowance of $1,000 (later reduced to $800) for a clerk; and $500 to pay for stationery, stamps, fuel to heat the office, and "a boy to attend to menial duties." Wirt also became the first attorney general to live full-time in Washington, D.C. Although this constant presence resulted in an increased workload, it wasn't until 1831 that Congress began giving the attorney general regular yearly appropriations for a messenger, furniture, books, and other office expenses.

appropriation: money authorized for a specific purpose

Also in 1831, John Berrien became the first attorney general who was asked to resign over a legal issue. President Andrew Jackson wanted to close the National Bank established during Washington's administration, and he asked Berrien to write an opinion allowing him to withdraw bank funds. Berrien refused, so Jackson replaced him with Roger Taney, who wrote the opinion that Jackson requested. After Treasury Secretary William Duane

John MacPherson Berrien (1781-1856) was the 10th attorney general of the United States. After resigning under pressure from President Jackson, he served more than a decade in the U.S. Senate.

refused to go along with the president's efforts to close the National Bank, he, too, was fired and replaced by Taney. The bank funds were finally withdrawn and the bank was closed. Jackson was censured by Congress for his actions, but he still set an example for future administrations: cabinet members served at the pleasure of the president, and he had the authority to replace whomever he chose.

In 1853, the attorney general's salary was increased to $8,000, finally equal to the pay of other department heads in the executive branch. When Caleb Cushing assumed the office that year, the attorney general became a full-time position; no longer would there be a private practice on the side. The duties and responsibilities of the office continued to expand, and Congress authorized the appointment of an assistant attorney general in 1859.

Several presidents had recommended centralizing all government legal work into one department, but Congress never acted for fear of infringing on the rights of the states.

censure: an official reprimand

Caleb Cushing (1800-1879), the 23rd attorney general, was the first to give up his private law practice.

litigation: engagement in legal proceedings; a lawsuit

During the Civil War, however, the office of the attorney general was so understaffed and overburdened that outside attorneys had to be hired to help with the workload. The cost for these private legal services was so expensive that Congress, in an effort to save money, finally supported the creation of a single law department, the Department of Justice, in 1870. The federal government was given centralized authority over federal litigation in the lower courts, and the attorney general controlled the coordination of legal policy.

The creation of the Department of Justice transformed the office of attorney general into a major administrative position. In addition to supervising all government litigation, the attorney general reviewed executive orders and proclamations, provided legal advice in the preparation of legislation, made recommendations to the president regarding pardons, and gave annual reports to Congress. As the attorney general's role expanded throughout the years, so did the Department of Justice. Additional departments and offices (such as the Office of Public Affairs, the Antitrust Division, and the Civil Rights Division) came under the administration of the attorney general as the Justice Department gradually developed into the modern, elaborate bureaucracy it is today.

By the turn of the twenty-first century, there had been almost 80 attorneys general, and all of them brought distinctive personality and policy traits to the office. Some made a great impact in their role as chief law-enforcement officer of the United States. A few made lasting contributions by furthering social reforms and civil rights. Still others violated individual liberties and abused the power of their office. *Attorneys General: Enforcing the Law* examines the lives and careers of eight attorneys general who were particularly exceptional during their time in the cabinet. William Wirt (attorney general from 1817 to 1829) institutionalized the office, formalized procedures, and defined the attorney general's role. During the Civil War, Edward Bates (1861-1864) wrote legal opinions sanctioning President Abraham Lincoln's use of emergency powers. A. Mitchell Palmer (1919-1921) abused his office for political gain, violating personal liberties and constitutional guarantees. During World War II, Francis Biddle (1941-1945) was torn between the demands of his president, Franklin D. Roosevelt, and his duty to protect the civil liberties of American citizens. Herbert Brownell (1953-1958) and Robert F. Kennedy (1961-1964) were both instrumental in civil rights reform and legislation. Scandal and controversy rocked the term of Edwin Meese III (1985-1988), who publicly attacked the Supreme Court and actively advanced the conservative policies of President Ronald Reagan. Janet Reno (1993-2001), the first woman to hold the office, dealt with a series of headline-making crises. The epilogue examines Reno's successor, John Ashcroft, and how the war on terrorism has affected the role of the attorney general.

The modern Department of Justice is organized into six major divisions, each headed by an assistant attorney general: Antitrust, Civil, Civil Rights, Criminal, Environmental and Natural Resources, and Tax.

★ ★ *1* ★ ★

WILLIAM WIRT

Defining the Office

At the same time that his book *Sketches of the Life and Character of Patrick Henry* was being published in 1817, the distinguished lawyer and author William Wirt was offered the position of United States attorney general by President James Monroe. Wirt, however, was more nervous and excited about his book than about his appointment to the president's cabinet. His insecurity surfaced when he wrote to Thomas Jefferson on August 24, 1816, "If you think the publication of the work will do me an injury with the public, I beg you to tell me so, without any fear of wounding my feelings." Despite only fair to mixed reviews from literary critics, Wirt was relieved when Jefferson stated, "Those who take up your book, will find they cannot lay it down," and John Adams declared it to be "rich entertainment."

As for the attorney general position, Wirt was frank when he wrote to his friend William Pope on January 18, 1818. "As to the office which I have received," Wirt declared, "it was not, trust me, either the supposed honor attached to it nor any ulterior promotion to which it might be supposed to lead, that induced my acceptance. No . . . it was the single object of bettering the fortunes of my children, by pursuing my profession on more advantageous ground."

Regardless of his motives, William Wirt served as attorney general for 12 years, longer than anyone else in

During his long term as the ninth U.S. attorney general, William Wirt (1772-1834) helped clarify the duties of the job for later officeholders.

the history of the office. He made a significant impact on the position by setting important precedents, as well as defining the responsibilities of the job. Although his biography of Patrick Henry is all but forgotten today, William Wirt is considered to be one of the first great attorneys general of the United States.

The Formative Years

Born on November 8, 1772, in Bladensburg, Maryland, William Wirt was the youngest of six children of Jacob and Henrietta Wirt. Within two years of William's birth, his father died, and his mother passed away shortly before his eighth birthday. From the age of seven, he lived with several families and attended a succession of boarding schools, where he studied the classics. He was a good student, enjoyed reading, and had a gift for public speaking. By the time he was 15, Wirt had used up his inheritance and began to rely on friends and benefactors to continue his education.

Benjamin Edwards, a former member of the Maryland legislature and the father of one of Wirt's classmates, was impressed with the intelligent and outgoing young man and invited him to live with his family. While Edwards advised and guided him in his studies, Wirt tutored Edwards's son and two cousins. It was Benjamin Edwards who urged him to make a career in law.

After almost two years with the Edwards family, Wirt became ill with tuberculosis and traveled to Georgia to stay with his sister Elizabeth. The Georgia climate helped him recover his health, and Wirt returned to Maryland to study law. About a year later, friends urged him to move to Virginia, where there were more opportunities for young lawyers. So Wirt moved to Fredericksburg, Virginia, and studied law under Thomas Swann, a former U.S. attorney. In 1792, at the age of 20, Wirt began his legal career at Culpeper County Courthouse, but clients were hard to come by. He supplemented his legal income by tutoring the children of leading families in the community, and in this way he made influential contacts.

In May 1795, 23-year-old Wirt married Mildred Gilmer, the daughter of Dr. George Gilmer, a prominent physician. Wirt moved in with his new wife at Pen Park, the home of his father-in-law, outside Charlottesville. The years at Pen Park were among Wirt's happiest. The handsome and friendly young lawyer became acquainted with Dr. Gilmer's distinguished circle of friends—including James Monroe, James Madison, and Thomas Jefferson. He perfected his skills in court and socialized late into the night. This happy existence ended abruptly with the death of his wife on September 17, 1799, after less than five years of marriage. Shaken by his loss, Wirt moved to Richmond to get a fresh start.

Wirt's friends urged him to run in the next election for clerk of the House of Delegates (part of the Virginia legislature), and he was elected with the help of his influential contacts. The position was prestigious, paying $145 a week for up to eight weeks of work each year. Wirt held the job for three legislative sessions, until 1802. He continued to take cases in his law practice, including some high-profile ones, and was regarded by many as an excellent young lawyer.

In 1802, Wirt's powerful friends in the Virginia legislature appointed him to be chancellor (judge) of the Tidewater District, which included all of Virginia southeast of Richmond. That same year, he met and married Elizabeth Gamble, the 17-year-old daughter of a wealthy Virginia merchant. With a new wife and soon a growing family (they eventually had 12 children together), Wirt resigned his position as chancellor and went back into private practice, where he could earn more money. He became partners with Littleton Waller Tazewell, who had a thriving law practice in Norfolk. The Wirts lived in Norfolk for two years; Wirt's law practice flourished, and his literary and legal reputation grew. Elizabeth was

William Wirt dabbled in literature throughout his career. In 1802 and 1803, a Richmond newspaper published a series of his essays, written in the form of a fictional Englishman's observations of America. They were so popular that they were published as a book called *The Letters of the British Spy*. Later, Wirt and several friends wrote a series of 33 essays called *The Old Bachelor*, published in the Richmond *Enquirer* between 1810 and 1813. Wirt wrote most of the pieces as the character of The Old Bachelor, who commented on subjects ranging from education to gambling to patriotism. This popular series was also published in book form, in several editions.

unhappy in the provincial seaport town, however, and the family moved back to Richmond in 1806.

In Richmond, Wirt became involved in two well-publicized cases that increased his status and fame. The first was in 1806, when he defended 17-year-old George Wythe Sweeney, who was charged with poisoning his 80-year-old great-uncle, George Wythe, and forging Wythe's name on six checks drawn on the Bank of Virginia. Wythe and one of his servants had died after drinking cups of coffee from the same pot. Wythe's cook, a former slave named Lydia Broadnax, had drunk the coffee and become violently ill, but she survived. She stated that she had seen Sweeney place a white substance in the coffeepot that morning, and arsenic was later found in the coffee grounds. Broadnax's testimony was not allowed in court, however, because Virginia law did not recognize testimony by a black witness

George Wythe (1726-1806) was a prominent lawyer and politician. His murder case was cause for gossip in Virginia, because it was widely believed that Lydia Broadnax was his mistress and the servant who died, Michael Brown, was in fact their son. In his will, Wythe had left them much of his property, with the remainder going to Sweeney. If Brown died before Sweeney, however, Sweeney would inherit everything. Resentful of having to share the inheritance, Sweeney decided to poison the entire household—but his plan ultimately backfired. Although Brown died immediately, Wythe survived long enough to change his will to exclude Sweeney completely.

against a white defendant. The rest of the evidence against Sweeney was circumstantial, and Wirt helped win his acquittal on the murder charges. Wirt's courtroom performance was praised in the Virginia newspapers.

Although he was primarily a defense attorney, Wirt was part of the prosecution team in the Aaron Burr conspiracy trial of 1807. Former U.S. vice president Aaron Burr had allegedly conspired to seize New Orleans and invade Mexico, creating a new, independent republic in the southwest territories over which he would rule. Indictments for treason were brought against Burr and a number of co-conspirators, including a wealthy Irishman named Harman Blannerhassett, who was to finance the scheme. When Judge John Marshall, who presided over the trial, limited what evidence could be presented to the jury, the case against Burr fell apart. Burr was found not guilty, but Wirt emerged from the trial a star. Especially memorable was his four-hour speech comparing Burr and Blannerhassett, which was considered a classic example of courtroom oration for many years. Wirt painted a picture of Blannerhassett as a harmless, scholarly man living peacefully on his quiet island paradise with his beautiful wife. According to Wirt, Burr entered the scene intent on corrupting the innocent Irishman and obtaining his wealth to finance treasonous schemes. Wirt's sensational orations were reported in newspapers throughout the country, making him a household name.

After the trial, Wirt's friend President Thomas Jefferson urged him to run for Congress and consider a life of public service. Wirt was flattered, but he declined the offer. In 1808, however, he was elected to a seat in Virginia's House of Delegates. He served for one term, then returned to his successful private law practice. When war broke out with Britain in 1812, Wirt turned down an army commission offered by President James Madison. When the British threatened an invasion of Richmond, however, Wirt raised a company of militia for the defense

circumstantial: not direct; secondary or incidental. Under the law, any evidence that is not eyewitness testimony is circumstantial.

acquit: to free or clear someone of a legal charge or accusation

prosecution: legal action initiated against a person; also, the lawyer or lawyers empowered to conduct such action on behalf of a government and its people

indictment: a formal statement that charges a person with a crime

The trial of Aaron Burr (1756-1836) brought together some of the most famous men of the time: the defendant was a former vice president, his defense team included great lawyers such as Edmund Randolph (the nation's first attorney general), and the judge was John Marshall, chief justice of the U.S. Supreme Court.

of the town. He was an artillery captain in command of a battalion, but saw no action in the war. In March 1816, Wirt was offered and accepted the position of U.S. attorney for the Richmond district. The job paid little and was essentially a part-time position that did not interfere with Wirt's thriving private practice.

In 1817, the 45-year-old attorney argued before the Supreme Court in a case that involved the property of a ship and its cargo. He made a four-and-a-half-hour speech to a packed courtroom. In a letter to his friend Judge Dabney Carr on February 27, Wirt wrote, "It makes me feel young again, and touches nerves that have been asleep ever since 1807. . . . Could I have supposed . . . that a day would ever come when I could dare to hold up my head in the Supreme Court of the United States, and take by the beard the first champions of the nation!" Less than a year later, Richard Rush resigned as attorney general to become ambassador to Great Britain, and President James Monroe asked Wirt to replace him. On November 13, 1817, William Wirt assumed the highest legal position in the land, becoming the lawful representative of the U.S. government in the Supreme Court.

In the Cabinet

When Wirt reported to work in January 1818, he was shocked to find there were no books, documents, or records of any kind from his predecessors. There was no clerk to assist him and no stationery. Wirt immediately bought office supplies at his own expense. His most important purchase was an opinion book, in which he began to keep a record of every official opinion he would give as attorney general. He wanted his successors to have the

Like William Wirt, James Monroe (1758-1831) was a lawyer from Virginia.

advantage of past records to provide uniformity in future decisions. Otherwise, their opinions might conflict with previous ones, causing the law to be interpreted inconsistently. (Eventually, in 1841, Congress began to collect and print the compiled opinions of the attorneys general.) Wirt also started a letter book, in which all his outgoing correspondence was copied. The record system he devised was continued until the paperwork began to be typed in the 1880s and was eventually bound into volumes.

Wirt was the first attorney general to officially establish a residence in Washington, D.C., and his presence led to an increased workload in the office. On March 27, 1818, he sent a letter to the chairman of the House Judiciary Committee detailing the problems he had encountered on the job and requesting expense money for a clerk and supplies. In 1819, Congress increased his salary to $3,500 and provided him with a grant of money for office expenses and a clerk.

One of the most important and lasting contributions that Wirt made was in defining the responsibilities of his position. The Judiciary Act of 1789 stated that the attorney general was to give legal opinions to the president and the heads of the departments in the executive branch (the secretaries of war, state, and treasury). But it had also become a courtesy over the years to give advice on constitutional matters to many others—committees of Congress, district attorneys, customs and tax officials, marshals, and even private citizens. This became an overwhelming burden for the part-time attorney general. So instead of expanding the scope of his job, Wirt decided to limit his duties to the exact letter of the law. He began denying his services to Congress and individuals. Even department heads were given opinions only on matters of law directly connected to the administration of their departments.

In January 1820, the House of Representatives requested an opinion by the attorney general on a petition. In a letter to the Speaker of the House, Wirt declined to give his opinion. He declared, "The attorney general is sworn to discharge the duties of his office according to law. To be instrumental in enlarging the sphere of his official duties beyond that which is prescribed by law would, in my opinion, be a violation of this oath. . . . Believing as I do that, in a government purely of laws, it would be incalculably dangerous to permit an officer to act, under color of his office, beyond the pale of the law, I trust that I shall be excused from making any official report on the order with which the House has honored me." Declining the House request put an end to providing legal advice to Congress.

While he was attorney general, Wirt was able to gain entrance to the Maryland bar, circumventing its strict requirements, and he built up a large private law practice in Baltimore and Annapolis. This was important, since Wirt depended on outside cases to subsidize his small government salary. Some in Congress considered this a conflict of interest, since he might represent a personal client in court one day, and then deal with the same client later as attorney general. Nothing came of these concerns, however, and over his 12 years as attorney general, Wirt was involved with several of the most famous Supreme Court cases in history.

conflict of interest: a clash between personal interests and official responsibilities of a person in an official position of trust

In *McCulloch v. Maryland* (1819), Wirt was back in the national spotlight, representing James W. McCulloch and the U.S. government in a power struggle with the state of Maryland. The case concerned the second national bank, which was established in 1816 (the charter of the first national bank had expired in 1811). It addressed several basic issues—whether Congress had the constitutional authority to incorporate a bank, whether the bank could open a branch in Baltimore without Maryland's consent, and whether Maryland had the right to tax the bank's revenues. McCulloch, a cashier at the national bank's Baltimore branch, had been charged with issuing money without paying the tax that Maryland required of a bank not chartered by the state.

*Founded "for the education
and instruction of Youth of
the Indian Tribes in this
Land . . . and also of English
Youth and any others,"
Dartmouth is the ninth oldest
college in the U.S. The
Supreme Court case would
decide whether it and other
private institutions could conduct their affairs without
state interference.*

Wirt argued that the first and second national banks
had already been lawfully established and the power to
create a bank "must be considered as ratified by the voice of
the people and sanctioned by precedent." The opposition
countered that the Constitution did not give Congress the
power to charter a bank, and that if the federal government
could tax state banks, then the state government could tax
the federal bank. The Supreme Court agreed with Wirt,
however, deciding in favor of the U.S. government. In his
written opinion, Chief Justice John Marshall declared the
bank lawful and constitutional, and he upheld that federal
law was supreme. The states, he wrote, had no power to
tax a national bank: "The whole might tax the part but the
part might not tax the whole."

In *Trustees of Dartmouth College v. Woodward* (1819),
Wirt represented the state of New Hampshire. Dartmouth
College had been established in 1769 with a charter
granted by King George III and the colonial governor of

New Hampshire. In 1816, the New Hampshire legislature revised the charter and created a new board of trustees in an attempt to place Dartmouth under state control. The original trustees sued and lost in the lower courts, but they won in the Supreme Court. Despite Wirt's arguments on behalf of the state, Chief Justice Marshall declared that the college was a private corporation, not a public one, and therefore it was protected from interference by the state. The original charter and board of trustees could not be changed by the state legislature.

States' rights were again in the spotlight in 1824 in the case of *Gibbons v. Ogden*. At issue was Congress' constitutional power to regulate interstate commerce. Aaron Ogden and Thomas Gibbons owned steamboat ferry lines that competed against each other to transport passengers across the Hudson River between Manhattan and the ports of New Jersey. Ogden's line operated under a monopoly (sole and exclusive control) granted by the state of New York, while Gibbons had a federal license. Claiming that his state monopoly took precedence over a federal license, Ogden sued Gibbons to force him to stop his competing ferry service. After Ogden won in the state courts, Gibbons appealed to the Supreme Court. Wirt argued for Gibbons against the state monopoly, and won the case. Justice Marshall, in delivering the court's opinion, stated that the New York monopoly interfered with the power of Congress to regulate interstate commerce, and it was therefore invalid and unconstitutional.

Although Wirt disliked the life of a public official, he stayed on as attorney general when the new president, John Quincy Adams, asked him to remain in 1824. When Adams's term ended in 1828, Wirt left public service after more than a decade in Washington.

Competing steamboat operators Thomas Gibbons (above; 1757-1826) and Aaron Ogden (1756-1839)

Looking Forward

Wirt continued to take on high-profile cases after leaving office. In 1830, he successfully defended Judge James Peck in a Senate impeachment hearing. In 1830 and 1831, he defended the constitutional rights of the Cherokee Indians against the state of Georgia.

Wirt disliked the new president, Andrew Jackson, and they were on opposite sides of many issues. Jackson had been a vocal supporter of Aaron Burr in 1807. He was an opponent of the national bank and rejected the Supreme Court's decision in *McCulloch v. Maryland*. Jackson vetoed the bank recharter bill in 1832, withdrew federal deposits in 1833, and effectively eliminated the bank. He also opposed Wirt and supported Georgia in its battle to take over Cherokee land. Wirt came to detest Jackson so much that he ran against him in the 1832 presidential election as a candidate for the Anti-Masonic Party. Wirt carried Vermont and received 40 percent of the vote in Pennsylvania, but Jackson won reelection by a landslide. Wirt died two years later, on February 18, 1834, at the age of 62.

In 1826, a man named William Morgan disappeared from New York State after writing a book about the Masons, a secret society. Although there was no proof, many people believed that the Masons had murdered Morgan (a former Mason) for revealing their secrets. The incident inspired so much opposition to the Masons that it eventually led to the formation of the Anti-Masonic Party. In addition to campaigning against any Masons running for public office, the party opposed Andrew Jackson and his policies. Wirt was its first and last presidential candidate; in 1834, the Anti-Masons helped form the new Whig Party.

William Wirt was a reluctant public figure, but during his long career as attorney general he shaped the responsibilities of the office for all those who came after him. He established a system of recording opinions and correspondence that gave future attorneys general the information necessary to ensure uniformity in their legal decisions. His well-written opinions and eloquent arguments set a standard of excellence for his successors. Never interested in political conflicts, Wirt confined his duties strictly to interpreting the law. As Secretary of State John Quincy Adams commented, "Mr. Wirt argued the point, as he naturally and properly does all questions in the cabinet, as a lawyer." Wirt's professionalism and neutrality became a model for attorneys general to follow. In the years to come, however, the position of attorney general became increasingly politicized, and many officeholders would find themselves involved in policymaking—and sometimes embroiled in controversy.

★ ★

Caleb Cushing: Expanding the Office

Unlike his predecessor William Wirt, who limited and defined the responsibilities of the attorney general, Caleb Cushing (1800-1879) expanded the scope and duties of the office. As the 23rd attorney general of the United States, serving from 1853 to 1857, he was an important and outspoken advisor to President Franklin Pierce and a supporter of proslavery positions up until the Civil War. An ambitious and forceful man, Cushing earned a reputation for getting things done in the Pierce cabinet.

When Cushing took office, the attorney general's salary was raised to $8,000, finally equal to other cabinet posts. Cushing voluntarily gave up his private law practice, moved to Washington, D.C., and became the first full-time attorney general. Congress increased his clerks to four and assigned additional duties to the attorney general's office, including advising treaty commissioners, examining land claims, administering government patents, and compiling and publishing federal laws. In 1856, Cushing obtained a special appropriation from Congress to hire temporary law assistants to handle hundreds of California land claims.

With the cooperation of the secretary of state, Cushing advised the president to transfer several of the State Department's functions to the office of the attorney general. These included pardons, legal appointments, official legal correspondence for other departments, extradition cases, and judicial appointments. The changes made the attorney general more important and powerful than ever before, and they also resulted in Cushing having a significant impact on executive decisions.

Cushing used his position to make policy within the Pierce administration. In particular, he wrote opinions in support of slavery and Southern interests because he believed this was the only way to preserve the Union. In an opinion strengthening the Fugitive Slave Law (which required citizens to aid federal authorities in returning slaves to their owners), he stated that a U.S. marshal could ask for help from the military in finding and keeping runaway slaves. In another opinion, Cushing wrote that the Missouri Compromise of 1820 (which defined whether new states would enter the Union as slave states or free states) was unconstitutional because it violated the rights of the states to decide the issue of slavery.

Cushing left behind a body of official opinions and legal precedents that filled three volumes. Highly partisan and political, he strengthened the office of attorney general and helped to make it equal in importance to the other executive departments.

★ ★

EDWARD BATES

War, Civil Liberties, and Slavery

In May 1860, Edward Bates of Missouri believed he would be nominated for president by the Republican Party. A Virginian by birth, Bates had many connections to the South, yet he was a well-known moderate who disliked slavery and opposed secession. He was a safe and acceptable choice for the presidency in most areas of the country. As delegates assembled in Chicago for the national convention, Bates's main competition seemed to be William Seward of New York. Neither Bates nor Seward viewed Abraham Lincoln, the candidate from Illinois, as a threat.

Supporters of Edward Bates were optimistic about his chances—until German American delegates discovered that he had been briefly affiliated with the American Party. Its members, known as "Know-Nothings," wanted to elect only native-born Americans and supported a 25-year residency requirement for citizenship. The German Americans objected to Bates's past connection to the Know-Nothings and rejected his candidacy. Meanwhile, Lincoln strategists busied themselves collecting second-ballot votes. These commitments to Lincoln, coupled with the anti-Bates feelings of the German delegates, turned the tide for the Illinois lawyer. Bates got 42 votes on the first ballot and only 35 votes on the second ballot while Lincoln gained strength. Seward's popularity dropped by the third ballot, and it was Lincoln, not Bates, who won the Republican nomination.

The 26th attorney general, Edward Bates (1793-1869), had to make tough decisions about the powers of the federal government when the United States was torn apart by the Civil War.

Crowds gathered to watch the Republican Party choose the second presidential candidate in its history. The party had formed just six years earlier, in 1854, to oppose slavery and its extension into the Western territories.

After Lincoln was elected president in November, he asked Edward Bates to be his attorney general. With the nation poised on the brink of civil war, Bates agreed. The first man west of the Mississippi to be appointed to the cabinet set off for Washington determined to help his country in any way possible during the crisis. As attorney general, Bates would become a key figure in controversial decisions by President Lincoln to restrict individual civil liberties during a time of war.

The Formative Years

Edward Bates was born in Goochland County, Virginia, in 1793. He was the youngest of 12 children of Thomas Bates—a Revolutionary War veteran—and his wife,

Caroline. When his father died in 1805, Edward went to live with an older brother, then later moved to the home of a cousin. An intelligent boy, he was tutored in philosophy, history, and science. He spent three years at the Charlotte Hall Academy in St. Mary's County, but preferred private tutoring to formal schooling.

When the War of 1812 broke out, Edward enlisted in the Virginia militia and served as a sergeant in a volunteer company. By the war's end in 1814, the 21-year-old decided to head west to join his older brother Frederick, who was a well-known judge and successful businessman in the frontier town of St. Louis in the Missouri Territory. Frederick encouraged Edward to pursue a career in law and public service.

Edward Bates began to study law with Frederick and a local attorney named Rufus Easton. By the end of 1816, he completed his legal studies and passed the bar exam. He made many contacts through his brother and started his own law practice, which included influential clients such as the territorial governor, officials from his administration, and other wealthy businessmen in the area. Bates's reputation as a gifted speaker and lawyer grew, and in 1818, the governor appointed him attorney for the Northern District of Missouri. Bates also played an active role in gaining statehood for Missouri. He entered politics as an elected delegate to the state constitutional convention in 1820 and was named by new governor Alexander McNair as Missouri's first state attorney general. In 1822, he was elected to the Missouri House of Representatives.

In 1823, Bates met and married Julia Coalter, with whom he would eventually have 17 children (although only 8 lived to adulthood). After the birth of their first child, he decided to forgo reelection, devoting himself to his family and his private law practice. He was appointed to the post of United States attorney and helped in his brother Frederick's successful race for governor. Frederick's term was short-lived, however; he died unexpectedly in August

1825 after a brief illness, leaving a great void in his brother's life.

Bates resumed his own political career in 1826, when he was elected to the U.S. House of Representatives. He ran for reelection two years later, but he was defeated. Returning home to Missouri, Bates was elected to the state Senate in 1830 and assumed leadership of those opposed to the political policies of President Andrew Jackson and his supporters. In 1834, Bates was elected to the Missouri House of Representatives and joined the Whig Party. Ill and discouraged, however, he returned to private practice after his one-year term. He still held a position of leadership within the Whig Party, but he settled into political retirement and concentrated on making money to support his wife and children.

In 1847, Bates was appointed by the Whig state central committee as a delegate to the U.S. River and Harbor Convention in Chicago. He agreed to attend and represent Missouri's interest in river improvement and mineral resources development. To his surprise, Bates was elected presiding officer of the convention, and he made a major speech focusing on national unity and western expansionism. He called for moderation and compromise on the issue of slavery and its extension into the territories, and he proposed building a transcontinental railroad. The Whig from Missouri impressed the delegates and gained national recognition at the convention.

In 1848, Bates supported the Whig candidate for president, Zachary Taylor. His campaign efforts strengthened the Whig Party in Missouri, and when Taylor was elected, there was talk of a cabinet position for Bates. The offer was never made, but after Taylor died in office in 1850, Millard Fillmore became president, and he reorganized the cabinet. By then Bates was the Whig Party spokesman in the West, and Fillmore offered him the position of secretary of war. Bates declined the honor. When Fillmore then offered him the secretary of the interior position, Bates turned him down again. He preferred to remain in Missouri and focus on Whig Party politics at the state level. This strategy seemed successful: when General Winfield Scott was selected as the Whig Party candidate in the presidential election of 1852, Bates received 97 votes on the first ballot in the vice presidential contest. He lost to William Graham on the second ballot, however, and Scott went on to lose the presidential election to Democrat Franklin Pierce.

In 1854, Bates aligned himself with the American Party in an attempt to bring Whigs and Know-Nothings together to oppose the extension of slavery. Bates even

GRAND, NATIONAL, WHIG BANNER.

This 1852 banner advertised Whig presidential candidate Winfield Scott and his running mate, William Graham. Even as it emphasized keeping the nation united—"No North, no South, no East, no West, nothing but the Union"—the Whig Party was being torn apart by internal differences and would dissolve within a few years.

Members of the American Party were called "Know-Nothings" because they were so highly secretive; when asked about their activities, they would reply that they knew nothing. The party was formed in the 1840s by people who opposed immigrants and foreigners in the United States. Eventually, the group was split apart by the slavery issue.

After seceding from the Union in December 1860, South Carolina demanded all federal property within the state, including the forts in Charleston harbor. President James Buchanan refused to evacuate Fort Sumter, as did Abraham Lincoln, who took office in March 1861. On April 12, Confederate forces began a 34-hour gun bombardment of the fort, and the 100-man federal force surrendered on April 14. The attack on Fort Sumter was the first battle of the Civil War.

considered a coalition of antislavery Democrats, Know-Nothings, and Whigs to support Millard Fillmore in 1856. That same year, he presided over the Whig National Convention in Baltimore, which nominated Fillmore as its candidate. The Whig Party platform did not address the slavery issue, however, and Bates became disillusioned. James Buchanan won the presidential election that year, and proslavery Democrats were elected throughout Missouri. Yet even though the defeated Whigs were falling out of power (and existence), Edward Bates was gaining national attention and support as a possible presidential candidate.

Once it became clear that Abraham Lincoln would be the Republican nominee for president in 1860, antislavery Whigs and Know-Nothings supported the Republican ticket and so did Edward Bates. Lincoln was elected, and on March 4, 1861, Bates took the oath of office as attorney general in Washington, D.C. At the age of 68, he would be the oldest cabinet member. His office, located in a wing of the Treasury Building on Pennsylvania Avenue, employed an assistant attorney general, six clerks, and a laborer.

In the Cabinet

There was no honeymoon period for the new cabinet. After Lincoln's victory, Southern states began to secede from the Union and form their own nation, the Confederate States of America. South Carolina was the first, on December 20, 1860, followed by the states of Mississippi, Florida, Alabama, Georgia, Louisiana, and Texas. On April 12, 1861, the Confederates fired on Fort Sumter in South Carolina and the Civil War officially began. President Lincoln immediately called up 75,000 militia troops and ordered a blockade of Southern ports. Virginia then seceded from the Union, but western Virginia declared itself separate from Virginia, formed a new state, and stayed within the Union. Finally, Arkansas, Tennessee, and North Carolina joined the Confederacy.

In the early days of the war, Washington, D.C., was considered to be at great risk of Confederate attack. There was widespread fear in the city, which was located just north of Virginia and just south of Maryland, a slave state that had not seceded. Troops were called to the capital to shore up its defenses. They had to pass through Maryland to get to Washington, since Baltimore was a major railroad junction. But Maryland—and especially Baltimore—had many Southern sympathizers, and Union leaders worried that the state would secede and join the Confederacy.

When the first companies of soldiers from Minnesota and Pennsylvania began to make their way through Baltimore, mobs stoned them and jeered at them. On April 19, the situation escalated. While a regiment of

Lincoln's cabinet in 1861. Its members were (from left to right) Postmaster General Montgomery Blair, Secretary of the Interior Caleb Smith, Secretary of the Treasury Salmon P. Chase, Lincoln, Secretary of State William Seward, Secretary of War Simon Cameron, Bates, and Secretary of the Navy Gideon Welles.

Massachusetts volunteers was being transported by horse-drawn wagons from one railroad station to another so they could travel on to Washington, a mob attacked the last two wagons with rocks. One wagon fled back to the station it had come from. Separated from their regiment by 20,000 angry people, the remaining 350 soldiers decided to fight their way ahead on foot. They fired into the crowd, and when the dust finally cleared, 4 soldiers and 12 civilians had been killed.

Members of the Sixth Regiment of Massachusetts Volunteers face off against angry Baltimore residents.

Fearing that more Northern troops would be sent through Baltimore, local officials burned several important railroad bridges. With Washington almost cut off

from the north, Lincoln began to consider a drastic step—the suspension of the right of habeas corpus. Habeas corpus protected prisoners from unlawful imprisonment by the government. Anyone arrested or detained could request a court to send a writ, or court order, to the official holding him or her in custody. The writ of habeas corpus required the official to explain to the court why the prisoner had been detained. The court would then determine whether the prisoner should be released or continue to be imprisoned. (The court did not decide whether the prisoner was guilty or not guilty, only whether he or she had been accorded due process of law.) Suspending this right would allow the Union to hold its opponents for as long as necessary without having to prove a cause.

Lincoln consulted Attorney General Bates, but there was no legal precedent for suspending habeas corpus. On April 27, 1861, believing that the situation was now critical, the president notified Winfield Scott, the commanding general of the Union Army, that "if at any point on or in the vicinity of any military line which is now or which shall be used between the city of Philadelphia and the city of Washington you find resistance which renders it necessary to suspend the writ of habeas corpus for the public safety, you personally, or through the officer in command at the point where resistance occurs, are authorized to suspend the writ."

Soon after Lincoln issued this order, an incident occurred challenging the suspension of habeas corpus. On May 25, a Maryland state legislator named John Merryman was imprisoned for participating in the destruction of railroad bridges in Baltimore. Merryman's lawyer drew up a petition for a writ of habeas corpus, and Chief Justice of the Supreme Court Roger B. Taney, also a judge in the circuit court of Maryland, issued the writ. On Lincoln's instructions, the arresting officer, General George Cadwalader, refused to release Merryman or to appear in court. Taney handed down a written opinion, which concluded that the

The writ of habeas corpus received its name from the Latin phrase *habeas corpus*, which means "produce the body," since a writ of habeas corpus orders the imprisoning official to bring the prisoner physically to court. The Founding Fathers thought habeas corpus was so important that they put it in the Constitution, which states, "The Privilege of the Writ of Habeas Corpus shall not be suspended, unless when in Cases of Rebellion or Invasion the public Safety may require it."

"Are all the laws, but one, to go unexecuted, and the government itself to go to pieces, lest that one be violated?"
—Abraham Lincoln, defending the suspension of habeas corpus

Roger Taney (1777-1864) served as attorney general before joining the Supreme Court in 1836.

jurisdiction: the authority to administer justice in a particular area

judicial review: examination of a government official or entity's actions by a court of law

John Merryman was indicted in July 1861 for conspiracy to commit treason. He was freed on bail, however, and his case was never brought to trial.

president did not have the power to suspend habeas corpus while civil courts were still functioning; only Congress had that power. Taney also stated that the military could not arrest and try a civilian, and President Lincoln had no power to give this authority to the military.

Bates, like Lincoln, believed that habeas corpus should be suspended in order to crush the Confederacy, and he began work on a written opinion that would justify the president's actions. He was cautious, however. He did not want to undermine executive authority in a time of civil war, but he had his own doubts about the power of the military in civilian jurisdictions. Bates stated that when the existence of the nation was threatened by "a great and dangerous insurrection," the president had the lawful power to arrest and hold in custody people who helped and supported the rebels. He explained that the president could not perform his duty of preserving the Constitution and executing the laws of the country without the power to oppose and suppress rebellions: "The President must, of necessity, be the sole judge, both of the exigency which requires him to act, and of the manner in which it is most prudent for him to employ the powers entrusted to him, to enable him to discharge his constitutional and legal duty— that is, to suppress the insurrection and execute the laws." The president had the power to suspend habeas corpus because he was charged with protecting the public safety. Furthermore, Bates declared that the president's decisions were not subject to judicial review and he was therefore not required to obey Taney's order in the Merryman case.

On March 3, 1863, Congress passed the Habeas Corpus Act, which officially gave the president the legal authority to suspend habeas corpus. Historians differ as to the number of military arrests of civilians without benefit of the writ of habeas corpus during the Civil War. Estimates range from 13,535 to 38,000, but the lack of records makes it impossible to verify these numbers. Many prisoners were released after a few months. Others were incarcerated

THE GRAVE OF THE UNION.
OR MAJOR JACK DOWNING'S DREAM. DRAWN BY ZEKE.

for the duration of the war. Some were banished to the Confederacy.

Although the suspension of habeas corpus was the most controversial issue while Bates was attorney general, Congress and the president during his first year added new responsibilities to the office, many of which were war-related. On August 2, 1861, Congress passed a bill giving the attorney general control over all the district courts and over the Treasury's payment of law-enforcement officers (previously, these had been duties of the Secretary of the Interior). Extra clerks were added to the attorney general's staff, and all U.S. attorneys and marshals were now to report to Bates.

Some Americans criticized the Habeas Corpus Act and other wartime measures that increased the government's power. Arguing that Lincoln and his administration were sacrificing civil liberties, this political cartoon portrayed government officials burying coffins labeled "Constitution," "Union," "Habeas Corpus," and "Free Speech & Free Press."

> **"T**here seems to be a general and growing disposition of the military, wherever stationed, to engross all power, and to treat the Civil Government . . . as if the object were to bring it into contempt."
> —Edward Bates, 1863

Bates was eager to end the Civil War for personal as well as political reasons. The conflict had divided his family; his son John served in the Union Army, while another son, Fleming, fought for the Confederacy. Fortunately, both survived the war.

This additional responsibility kept the attorney general extremely busy, especially as the federal government's legal functions kept expanding. On July 31, Congress had passed the Conspiracies Act, which called for district or circuit court trials of those who were accused of trying to overthrow the government. On August 6, an act of Congress called for federal prosecution of anyone who solicited recruits for the Confederate Army. On August 16, a presidential proclamation authorized federal marshals and attorneys to seize and condemn Confederate vessels. Congress also passed the Confiscation Bill, which allowed for legal seizure of property used in an effort to overthrow the government. Bates was in charge of prosecuting cases under these new laws, but he remained vigilant about asserting military power over civilians. For instance, he required concrete proof to prosecute people under the Confiscation Bill. Even for people who had clearly rebelled against the Union, evidence that their property had been used in planning an attack or in helping enemy soldiers was necessary before the federal government could seize their homes, livestock, or other belongings.

Although Bates was intensely loyal to Lincoln and the Union cause, he often disagreed with the president and other cabinet members on the issue of civil rights for black Americans. He endorsed Lincoln's 1863 Emancipation Proclamation as an essential step to preserve the Union, but he opposed the president's decision to enlist blacks in the military. He believed that, rather than working for the "civil and political equality of whites and Negroes," the federal government should resettle freed slaves in other parts of the world. His official opinions as attorney general, however, often contrasted with his personal beliefs.

For example, Bates rendered a favorable opinion in November 1862 regarding the citizenship of a ship captain who was a free black man. In 1821, Attorney General William Wirt had declared that a black slave in Virginia was not a U.S. citizen, because national citizenship

depended on state citizenship and Virginia law did not consider slaves to be citizens. In 1857, Supreme Court Chief Justice Roger Taney wrote in his opinion on *Scott v. Sandford* that under the Constitution no African American could become a U.S. citizen. Bates, however, determined that a citizen of any state of the United States was a member of the nation and that all people born in the U.S. or naturalized by law were citizens—including the ship captain. He declared that black citizens were as entitled to the protection of the national government as any other citizen: "the free man of color . . . if born in the United States, is a citizen of the United States, and if otherwise qualified, is

In July 1862, the Second Confiscation Act empowered the president to send ex-slaves and other blacks into combat, and Lincoln began doing so in July 1863. Posters like this one encouraged enlistment in all-black regiments of the Union Army.

Dred Scott (c.1795–c.1858) was a slave in Missouri. From 1833 to 1843, however, he lived with his owner in Illinois and the Wisconsin Territory, where slavery was outlawed. Upon his return to Missouri, he brought a case to court arguing that living in these areas made him a free man. After being unsuccessful in the state courts, he appealed to the Supreme Court in Scott v. Sandford. *Although he lost, Scott's case increased opposition to slavery in the North.*

amnesty: a pardon for past offenses

disenfranchise: to deprive a person of the right to vote

competent, according to the acts of Congress, to be master of a vessel engaged in the coasting trade." (Bates's opinion did not mean that blacks were entitled to the right to vote or hold office. He believed that these privileges were not essential to citizenship, pointing out that women and children were U.S. citizens and yet did not have them.)

In 1864, Bates was confronted with a petition from a chaplain in a black regiment in Massachusetts who applied for pay and allowances equal to white soldiers. Though Bates opposed blacks in the military, he realized they were still soldiers fighting for the Union cause. He concluded that the black soldiers were entitled to the same payment that white soldiers received. Following Bates's recommendation, Congress passed a bill on June 15 providing equal pay for black soldiers.

As the war wound down, President Lincoln and his cabinet discussed how to treat the defeated Confederacy. Bates believed in universal amnesty for Southerners and a return of full property and political rights to former Confederates once the war was over. These views clashed with those of the military commanders and of the radical Republicans in Congress, who wanted to punish the South. Bates gradually began to be isolated from others in the cabinet, and eventually from President Lincoln.

His health failing, the 71-year-old attorney general decided to leave the cabinet after Lincoln's reelection in 1864. The president offered Bates a district court judgeship in western Missouri, but he declined, hoping to be appointed instead to the U.S. Supreme Court (Chief Justice Taney had just died, leaving a vacancy). The president bypassed him, however, and appointed Salmon P. Chase instead. Disappointed, Bates returned home to Missouri.

Bates found the same issues in his native state that he had left behind in Washington. Radical Republicans who supported martial (military) law in Missouri had called for a state convention to create a new constitution that would abolish slavery and disenfranchise those who fought for the South. Bates became a strong critic of this group, and he published a series of newspaper articles in the *Missouri Democrat* detailing his opinions. In the articles, Bates opposed martial law and advocated gradual progress in obtaining rights for blacks, rather than granting them immediate suffrage. When the convention voted to adopt the new constitution on April 8, 1865, Bates fought against ratification. But the radical Republicans won a narrow victory in the election and the constitution was certified. When these same Republicans were successful in the 1866 elections, Bates retired from politics.

Looking Forward

Bates was consistent to the end of his life in his views on military authority. After the assassination of Abraham Lincoln on April 14, 1865, Bates's successor, Attorney General James Speed, issued a one-sentence opinion. The shortest in the history of the office, it declared the legality of trying Lincoln's assassins before a military commission instead of in the civil courts. Bates angrily denounced Speed for supporting military trials for civil offenses. "I cannot help pitying my poor imbecile successor," declared Bates. "Such a trial is not only unlawful, but it is a gross blunder in policy: it denies the great fundamental principle, that ours is a government of *law*, and that the law is strong enough, to rule the people wisely and well." Bates even wrote a letter to President Andrew Johnson in 1866 suggesting that he issue an executive order to dissolve all military courts and end martial law.

Edward Bates died on March 25, 1869, at the age of 76. His tenure as attorney general will be primarily remembered for his opinion supporting Lincoln's suspension of habeas corpus, a controversy that is still debated to this day. Bates's opinions as a wartime attorney general in support of the president established a legal precedent for future holders of the office when faced with issues of civil liberties in times of upheaval and war.

In his famously brief opinion on Lincoln's assassins, James Speed (1812-1887) wrote simply: "SIR: I am of the opinion that the persons charged with the murder of a President of the United States can be rightfully tried by a military court."

★ ★ *3* ★ ★

A. MITCHELL PALMER

Abusing the Office

On June 2, 1919, United States Attorney General Alexander Mitchell Palmer spent most of the evening in the library of his fashionable home on R Street in Washington, D.C. At around 11:00 P.M., he went upstairs with his wife. Suddenly, about 15 minutes later, Palmer heard a loud thud near the front door and then an ear-splitting explosion. The entire front of the house had been destroyed by a bomb blast that surely would have killed or injured Palmer and his wife had they been downstairs. The explosion was so strong that it blew out the windows of neighbors' homes on the block, including those of Assistant Secretary of the Navy Franklin D. Roosevelt, who lived across the street.

Roosevelt rushed over to help, and he and Palmer searched around outside to see if they could find any clues. What they found were the shattered remains of a body, leading the authorities to believe that the explosion had gone off sooner than the bomber had expected. They also found scattered copies of an anarchist pamphlet, which stated, "There will have to be bloodshed; we will not dodge; there will have to be murder; we will kill, because it is necessary; there will have to be destruction; we will destroy to rid the world of your tyrannical institutions."

Attorney General Palmer wasn't the only target that night. Bombs exploded within the hour in seven other

Nationwide fear and hysteria fueled the tenure of 50th attorney general A. Mitchell Palmer (1872-1936), who ultimately went too far in his effort to protect the United States from threat.

45

Outside the Palmer home after the bomb explosion

anarchist: an opponent of all forms of political authority

communist: a supporter of a theoretical political and economic system based on government ownership of property

cities, destroying buildings and killing two people. A mayor, a state legislator, three judges, two businessmen, a policeman, and a Catholic priest were among the intended victims. Horrified and shaken by this obviously organized attempt to attack American institutions, Palmer took a strong stand against extremists. He marshaled all the forces of the Justice Department to find, punish, and deport anarchists, communists, and any other radicals who might threaten the American way of life. But along the way, he endangered the very liberties that he set out to defend.

The Formative Years

The third child of Samuel and Caroline Palmer, Alexander Mitchell Palmer was born near Stroudsburg, Pennsylvania,

on May 4, 1872. The Palmers made their living in con-
struction. They were devout Quakers and ardent
Democrats, though Pennsylvania at the time of Mitchell's
boyhood was a heavily Republican state. Of the six Palmer
children, young Mitchell was especially intelligent, and he
graduated number one in his class at Stroudsburg High
School at the age of 14.

After a year of college preparation at Moravian
Parochial School, Palmer enrolled at Swarthmore College,
a Quaker school near Philadelphia. A skillful writer and
orator, Palmer was known for his prizewinning speeches
and the ability to project his voice to large crowds. After
once again graduating first in his class, he returned to
Stroudsburg and embarked upon a career in law and
Democratic politics.

Palmer began studying law as a clerk in the office of
John B. Storm, a former congressman and local attorney.
When Palmer was admitted to the bar in 1893, Storm
made him a junior partner in the firm. After Storm was
appointed to a judgeship, Palmer took over the law practice
and became one of the leading attorneys in the county. In
1898, he married Roberta Bartlett Dixon, the daughter of
a wealthy Maryland businessman.

Palmer aspired to political office, and in 1900, he was
elected president of the Stroudsburg Democratic Club and
a member of the county's Democratic executive committee.
As a reform Democrat who favored women's suffrage and
child labor laws, he was elected to the U.S. House of
Representatives in 1909. Thanks to his speaking ability and
charisma, Palmer quickly rose to power during his four
years in the House. He was appointed to the important
Ways and Means Committee, which controlled committee
assignments. In 1910, he became head of the Democratic
Party in Pennsylvania, a position he held until 1921.
Palmer worked tirelessly for Democratic candidates, and by
1912, he had become one of the most influential men in the

incumbent: a person currently holding an office

party and one of the original supporters of Woodrow Wilson for the presidency.

Palmer worked hard for Wilson, ensuring that Pennsylvania's 52 Wilson delegates were elected in the state's presidential primary. As Wilson's floor leader at the national convention, Palmer was instrumental in gaining the presidential nomination for him. Palmer campaigned nonstop for Wilson in the election of 1912, and even though Pennsylvania went to the third-party candidate, Theodore Roosevelt, Wilson was elected president. Palmer was reelected to a third term in Congress, but he set his sights on a position in Wilson's cabinet, preferably the attorney general. Instead, President Wilson offered him the job of secretary of war. Palmer declined, stating that his Quaker antiwar beliefs would hinder him in the War Department. Instead, he remained in the House, working on social-welfare legislation.

Palmer still had ambitions of achieving higher office, however. He wanted to run for governor of Pennsylvania in 1914, but Wilson convinced him to run for the Senate opposing a powerful incumbent Republican, Boies Penrose. After a hard-fought campaign, Palmer lost to Penrose. Deeply disappointed with his defeat, he decided to retire from politics, and Wilson appointed him to a judgeship.

Ever the loyal Democrat and Wilson supporter, Palmer campaigned successfully for the president's reelection in 1916. When America entered World War I against Germany in 1917, Wilson appointed Palmer to the new position of alien property custodian, whose job was to take over and administer enemy-owned property. There were extensive German holdings in the United States; Palmer's office of 300 employees oversaw 30,000 trusts worth $800 million and supervised a wide range of German-American businesses, including farming, lumber, shipbuilding, mining, and manufacturing companies. The position helped Palmer expand his political base. He gained many allies by granting them jobs in the businesses he administered in exchange for their future support. Palmer focused his efforts on winning the Democratic presidential nomination in 1920. In March 1919, however, Thomas Watt Gregory retired as attorney general, and Wilson named A. Mitchell Palmer as his successor.

In the Cabinet

The mood of the country in 1919 was one of fear and paranoia. The economy was troubled by rising prices, shortages of goods, and a lack of jobs for soldiers coming home from the war. Struggling to make ends meet, many workers demanded better pay. When they were refused, labor unions went on strike. In 1919 alone, there were about 3,600 strikes in the United States, involving 4 million workers. The strikes paralyzed entire cities, leaving them

Woodrow Wilson (at head of table) with Palmer (second from left) and the rest of his cabinet

socialist: a supporter of a political system in which the means of producing and distributing goods and services is either owned collectively or owned by a government that plans and controls the economy

Basing their actions on the doctrines of Karl Marx, the Bolsheviks (headed by Vladimir Lenin) advocated the overthrow of the Russian tsar's government and the establishment of a dictatorship of the proletariat (working classes). They were successful in the 1917 Russian Revolution and became the Russian Communist Party in 1918.

The League of Nations, an international organization established by the peace treaties that ended World War I, was strongly supported by Woodrow Wilson. The United States was not a member of the League, however, because the Senate refused to ratify the Treaty of Versailles, bitterly disappointing Wilson.

without necessary services. Mob violence erupted across the nation. Many Americans blamed all their economic and social problems on the "radicals," a catchall term that lumped together communists, socialists, anarchists, left-wingers, and even striking trade unionists. Some Americans were afraid that these radical groups would begin a revolution, as the Bolsheviks (communists) had done in Russia two years before. Most people believed that all radicals wanted nothing short of a complete overthrow of the United States government and an end to the democratic way of life.

When A. Mitchell Palmer entered the cabinet in 1919, President Woodrow Wilson was more concerned with negotiating the peace treaty ending World War I and establishing the League of Nations than with the economic problems and mood of anxiety within the country. After Wilson suffered an incapacitating stroke later that year, it was Palmer who filled the leadership void and took control in dealing with the problems of labor unrest. As a member of the House of Representatives, Palmer had been a friend to labor, but as attorney general he became an opponent. He listened to the frightened public, which favored government intervention to stop the strikes.

Many Americans thought that radicals exerted strong influence over the labor unions and were responsible for the strikes. There were several radical groups in the U.S. at that time, including the socialists and the Industrial Workers of the World. With the success of the Bolshevik revolution in Russia, the communists (often known as "reds") were also in the spotlight. In 1919, there were about 70,000 members of the Communist and Communist Labor parties in the U.S. There were also nearly 500 radical newspapers or magazines advocating the overthrow of the American capitalist system. What most people did not understand, however, was that the radical movement was composed of many different groups whose goals and methods varied widely. They were often too poorly led and too deeply divided to work together for a common cause. Not only were the radicals less organized than people feared but, in addition, many so-called radicals were not really revolutionaries. Some were labor union members who simply wanted to improve their working conditions; others were progressive liberals and reformers.

A general strike began in Seattle, Washington, on February 6, 1919, and incapacitated the city. Federal troops were called in to stop the strike, which ended on February 11. Then, around May Day (May 1), a bomb plot to assassinate 36 of the most influential and famous men in America was uncovered. Palmer himself was on the hit list that included industrialists, businessmen, and government officials. The only serious casualty, however, was the maid of former U.S. Senator Thomas Hardwick of Georgia. She lost both of her hands when a small, rectangular package addressed to her employer exploded as she opened it. Also on May 1, rioting broke out in major U.S. cities—including New York, Boston, and Cleveland—when bystanders attacked various radical groups as they marched in May Day parades.

Newspapers fueled the nation's fear and panic with sensational headlines such as "TERROR REIGNS IN MANY CITIES" and "REDS PLANNED MAY DAY MURDERS." Police launched a huge investigation of the bomb plot, but no suspects were found. Pressure increased on the attorney general to take action against the apparent radical threat. The *New York Times* declared on May 4, "The policy of tolerance which has marked the attitude of the Department of Justice . . . must be dropped for one of vigorous prosecution if the Bolshevist movement is to be held in check."

After further bombings occurred on June 2—including the one at his own home—Palmer responded by declaring war on American radicalism. Congress gave the Justice Department an additional $500,000 to hunt down dangerous radicals. Palmer appointed Francis P. Garvan, a famous

The Industrial Workers of the World (IWW) was a radical wing of the American labor movement that wanted to unite all skilled and unskilled workers in one great union. The IWW's goal was to overthrow capitalism and build a socialist society.

May Day, the first day of May, was considered a holiday for labor and an occasion for parades, speeches, and demonstrations.

detective, as assistant attorney general in charge of investigating all radical activity. Palmer then made William J. Flynn, former head of the Secret Service, chief of the Bureau of Investigation. On August 1, Palmer created the General Intelligence Division (GID), whose only function was to collect information about radicals. He appointed 24-year-old J. Edgar Hoover (the future FBI director) to run the division.

That summer and autumn, the number of strikes increased and so did the violence. During a police strike in Boston between September 9 and September 12, criminals ran rampant and the state militia was activated to keep order. There was a nationwide steel strike in September, followed by a coal strike in November. The result was

After getting his start at the Justice Department under Palmer, John Edgar Hoover (1895-1972) took charge of the Federal Bureau of Investigation in 1924 and ran it until his death 48 years later. Hoover made the FBI more famous as well as more efficient, but he became best known for pursuing gangsters in the 1920s and 1930s and communists in the 1950s. Like Palmer, however, he was often criticized for abusing his position.

increased public fear and unrest, bordering on panic. The time seemed to have come for the government to take action, and Palmer seized center stage. As he later testified before a Senate committee, "I was urged . . . throughout the country to do something and do it now, and do it quick, and do it in a way that would bring results to stop this sort of thing in the United States."

Investigating and prosecuting actual crimes committed by radicals would be a slow, difficult, and possibly unsuccessful process. Instead, Palmer decided to concentrate on simply finding and deporting radicals, since 90 percent of them were foreign-born non-citizens. Deporting someone was an administrative process that did not require a jury trial, so it would allow Palmer to work around normal

Before child labor laws, young boys often worked alongside men in the coal mines.

legal procedures and would guarantee him quicker, more impressive results. Palmer used the Immigration Act of 1917 (amended in 1918) as the basis for his actions. This act stated that any alien anarchist could be deported from the country. Also, any alien who advocated violence against property, officials, or the government—or belonged to any organization that did—could be arrested and deported. Since arrest warrants and deportation orders could by law only come from the secretary of labor, the attorney general worked closely with Labor Secretary William B. Wilson in carrying out what historians refer to as the Palmer raids.

warrant: a document authorizing an official to perform a specific act, such as ordering a payment of funds, conducting a search, or performing an arrest

The first raid took place on the night of November 7, 1919, the second anniversary of the Russian Revolution. Russian radicals were targeted in 12 cities across the nation. Most of the arrests occurred at the main headquarters of

★ ★

The Red Scare

In 1919-1920, widespread anxiety over communists (often called "reds" after the color of the Bolshevik flag) came to be known as the "Red Scare."

During the Red Scare, ultra-patriotic societies like the American Legion were founded to foster "100% Americanism." In some places, Legionnaires held mock loyalty trials, ran all suspicious radicals out of town, or even tarred and feathered foreign-born residents. The membership of the Ku Klux Klan also increased dramatically. In an attempt to foster patriotism and pure Americanism, the Klan lumped together and denounced all foreigners, Catholics, blacks, and Jews.

Even individual Americans who were not members of such groups resorted to violence against aliens and suspected radicals. On May 6, 1919, a man who was attending a pageant in Washington, D.C., did not stand up and remove his hat during the playing of the national anthem. A sailor in the Navy took offense at this, pulled out a gun, and shot him three times in the back. The surrounding crowd then burst into cheers and applause. That same year, another man killed an alien for yelling "To hell with the United States." A jury acquitted the killer after only two minutes of deliberation. Fear and intolerance seemed to have replaced reason and justice in America.

★ ★

Copyrighted 1919 by The Philadelphia Inquirer Company

PUT THEM OUT AND KEEP THEM OUT

----Morgan in the Philadelphia Inquirer

This newspaper's political cartoon expressed the sentiments and fears of many Americans in 1919.

the Russian Workers Union in New York City. Nearly 200 people were arrested, even though Justice Department officials and police had only 27 warrants. Many of those arrested were beaten and mistreated during the raid. Some were American citizens; others had no connection to the Russian Workers Union. Even a few unlucky bystanders who happened to walk by during the raid were arrested. Beatings and arrests without warrants also occurred in other cities. Some Russians were imprisoned in Hartford, Connecticut, for five months without a hearing. On November 8, state and local officials followed Palmer's lead and raided 73 radical centers in New York City, arresting more than 500 people. Fewer than half of the hundreds

Of the 249 people deported to Russia on the Buford, *most had no criminal records and had never participated in any terrorist acts. Twelve of the men were forced to leave behind their wives and children in the United States. One of the prisoners was a woman—Emma Goldman (1869-1940), a famous anarchist and feminist.*

arrested in the federal and various local raids were finally judged to be deportable radicals.

Despite these obvious violations of civil liberties and the small numbers of radicals actually charged with crimes, Palmer enjoyed the complete support of the press and the public. When the army transport ship *Buford*, nicknamed the "Soviet ark," sailed to Russia on December 21, 1919, carrying 249 radicals away from the United States, the national press was full of praise. Guarded by 250 soldiers, the group of radicals was described as "the unholiest cargo that ever left our shores." Palmer promised Americans more Soviet arks to rid the country of dangerous radicals.

Buoyed by the praise he was receiving, Palmer planned larger raids and picked the communists as his next target. Armed with 3,000 warrants issued by the Department of

Labor, federal officials carried out a second Palmer raid on January 2, 1920, in 33 cities in 23 different states. More than 4,000 people were arrested, many without warrants. (In Massachusetts, 39 men were arrested for simply being in the wrong place at the wrong time. They had gotten together to form a cooperative bakery and made the mistake of gathering in a place often used by radicals.) There were more beatings and brutality, as well as mistreatment in detention centers, which were overcrowded and unsanitary. Some aliens were detained for long periods of time without hearings.

With arrests in the thousands and countless civil rights violations, some protests began to emerge. Francis Fisher Kane, U.S. attorney in Philadelphia, resigned in protest. The liberal press continued to criticize Palmer, and even a few mainstream newspapers questioned whether the raids were appropriate. In March 1920, Assistant Secretary of Labor Louis F. Post became acting labor secretary due to William Wilson's illness. Post took charge of all deportation cases from the January 2 raid. An expert on immigration law and procedure, Post reviewed each case in detail and discovered disturbing irregularities in the arrests that had been made. He canceled warrants where there was insufficient evidence, dismissed cases where there was illegally seized evidence, and ordered the release of those for whom there were no warrants. In the end, Post freed about 70 percent of those apprehended in the Palmer raids.

Palmer, who had just announced his campaign for the presidency, was infuriated with Post and called him a Bolshevik. After complaints from the Justice Department, the House of Representatives began impeachment hearings against Post in May. One week before Post's testimony was to begin, Palmer predicted another violent May Day for America, warning of strikes, bombings, and even assassinations of prominent officials. State militias and federal troops were on the alert and anxiety mounted, but May 1 came and nothing happened. This time, Palmer bore the

Post found that, of the thousands arrested in the Palmer raids, only 40 claimed they wanted to overthrow the government, and only 3 actually possessed guns. Most of the arrested aliens, he said, were "wage workers, useful in industry, good-natured in their dispositions, unconscious of having given offense. Very few, if any, were the kind of aliens that Congress could in all reasonable probability have intended to comprehend in its anti-alien legislation."

"I apologize for nothing that the Department of Justice has done in this matter. I glory in it. I point with pride and enthusiasm to the results of that work; and if . . . some of my agents . . . were a little rough or unkind, or short and curt, with these alien agitators, whom they observed seeking to destroy their homes, their religion and their country, I think it might well be overlooked in the general good to the country which has come from it."
—A. Mitchell Palmer

brunt of the criticism. The press accused him of seeing radicals everywhere. During Post's testimony before Congress, the articulate and intelligent assistant labor secretary gave examples of mistaken arrests and charged the Justice Department with abuse. This, coupled with Palmer's unfounded May Day threats, turned public opinion against the attorney general.

By spring 1920, the "Red Scare" anxiety had eased throughout the United States. The economy improved, labor strikes decreased, and the public lost interest in the supposed radical threat. Palmer, however, continued to warn of danger from radicals. He was investigated by several congressional committees. The same newspapers that had once praised him now condemned him as an alarmist. Some accused him of trying to capitalize politically on the Red Scare. He was detested by organized labor. By the time the national party convention was held in 1920, most Democrats thought Palmer was a weak candidate who

Palmer, despite his best efforts, lost political support after the Red Scare subsided.

couldn't win in November. Although he had the backing of many state politicians and party regulars, he withdrew his candidacy after the 38th ballot. His political career at an end, Palmer finished out his term as attorney general in relative quiet, then retired to his home in Pennsylvania.

Looking Forward

Palmer had a heart attack in 1922 and suffered from poor health throughout the remainder of his life. He made a few campaign speeches on behalf of Democratic presidential candidates in 1924 and 1928. His friendship with his former neighbor, Franklin D. Roosevelt, continued. Roosevelt called on his old friend in 1932 to help write the Democratic Party platform to be used in his presidential campaign. Palmer gladly obliged, and his draft was adopted by the national convention in Chicago. After Roosevelt was elected, Palmer visited him at the White House, but in the next few years he grew disillusioned with the president's liberal policies. Palmer died of a final heart attack on May 11, 1936, at the age of 64.

In American history, the name of A. Mitchell Palmer will always be associated with the Red Scare, the Palmer raids, and the violation of civil liberties. To his credit, Palmer did not initiate the panic over radicals, and he resisted taking action until pressure from the public and the press grew intense. The drastic action he took was what the people clamored for, but as historian Stanley Coben suggests, "a leading government official has a higher duty than giving the public—or his party—what it wants." In his zeal to enhance his own political career, Palmer was happy to exploit public emotion and cast himself as a hero protecting his country. He was not the first attorney general to place politics ahead of the law, and he would not be the last. He was also not the first or last to be faced with the decision to sacrifice individual liberties—particularly those of racial or ethnic minorities—in the name of a national emergency.

$\star$ $\star$ *4* $\star$ $\star$

FRANCIS BIDDLE

Loyalty versus Conscience

Two framed pictures hung on the wall of Francis Biddle's study. One was an engraving of George Washington's first cabinet, which had only four members: Secretary of War Henry Knox, Secretary of the Treasury Alexander Hamilton, Secretary of State Thomas Jefferson, and Attorney General Edmund Randolph. Randolph, the first attorney general, was Biddle's great-great-grandfather on his mother's side. The picture of him always reminded Biddle of his historical links to democracy and law. The other picture was a photograph of Franklin D. Roosevelt's cabinet, which consisted of 11 individuals—one of whom was Francis Biddle.

Biddle's relationship with Roosevelt began early in his life, at the Groton School in Massachusetts. When Biddle entered Groton as a shy 13-year-old schoolboy in 1899, Roosevelt, four years older, was a confident, outgoing, and handsome upperclassman. He was "a magnificent but distant deity, whose splendor added to my shyness," recalled Biddle in his autobiography. Biddle's deference and respect toward Roosevelt continued into adulthood. In 1943, Roosevelt was introducing his cabinet to Madame Chiang Kai-Shek of China, America's ally in the war against Japan. When it was Biddle's turn to be introduced, the president said, "I was a sixth former at school when the attorney general was a second former. . . . He hasn't forgotten it."

The 58th attorney general, Francis Biddle (1886-1968), had to decide whether national security during World War II was worth abridging the individual rights of some American citizens.

Telling the story later, Biddle added, "He smiled, with a little tightening of the lips, to make sure I should get the point of reference."

In the course of his tenure as attorney general, Francis Biddle opposed the actions taken by Roosevelt's administration against Japanese Americans during World War II. At the time, Biddle was criticized for opposing the policy, and later he was condemned for not opposing it enough. His experience was a reminder that although the attorney general can give his or her advice and opinions on questions of law, it is the president who makes the final decision. Ultimately, an attorney general serves at the pleasure of the president. Such is the dilemma of any cabinet member—to support the president and at the same time follow his or her own conscience.

The Formative Years

Francis Beverly Biddle was born in Paris on May 9, 1886, while his parents were living in Europe. His mother, Frances, was descended from the Virginia Randolphs and Robinsons. His father, Algernon Sydney Biddle, was a law professor at the University of Pennsylvania in Philadelphia. Algernon died in 1891, when Francis was just five years old.

One of four brothers, Francis Biddle was educated at Haverford Academy from 1895 to 1899 and the Groton School from 1899 to 1905. He earned a B.A. from Harvard University in 1909, attended Harvard Law School, and then found his first job—as a personal secretary to Supreme Court Justice Oliver Wendell Holmes for the year 1911-1912. Holmes was a great influence on Biddle, instilling in him a sense of liberalism that continued throughout his life.

liberalism: a set of political or social beliefs that emphasizes reform, progress, tolerance, and protection of civil liberties through the actions of government

Biddle next moved to Philadelphia, was admitted to the Pennsylvania bar, and practiced law there for many years. He became interested in the Progressive Party of Theodore Roosevelt, working as a volunteer in Roosevelt's 1912 presidential campaign. Biddle was also a delegate to the party's 1916 convention; he was disappointed when

Roosevelt declined another presidential nomination, and like most Progressives, he supported the Republican candidate, Charles Evans Hughes. In 1918, during World War I, Biddle joined the army and trained to be an artillery officer, but the war ended before he could be activated. That same year he married Katherine Garrison Chapin, a successful poet with whom he would have two sons. From 1922 to 1926, Biddle served as a special assistant to the U.S. attorney for the Eastern District of Pennsylvania.

Like many wealthy and educated people of his day, Biddle was raised as a Republican. It was the Great Depression that changed his views and his party affiliation. "I saw the dark and dismal conditions under which the miners lived; and the brutality that was dealt them if they tried to improve things," Biddle wrote. He began working actively on behalf of workers' rights, representing Pennsylvania miners in court. In the 1932 election, Biddle switched allegiance from Republican President Herbert Hoover to Democratic candidate Franklin Roosevelt, who was more sympathetic to labor.

Roosevelt won the presidency, and Biddle's legal success soon impressed the Democrats in Washington. In 1934, President Roosevelt appointed Biddle to the chairmanship of the National Labor Relations Board, which helped employers and employees negotiate agreements to resolve labor disputes. Biddle served until 1935, and then returned briefly to his law practice in Philadelphia. In 1938, he was asked to be chief counsel in a congressional investigation into charges of corruption at the Tennessee Valley Authority (TVA), an organization that had been one of the Roosevelt administration's greatest achievements. Under Biddle's leadership, the charges were disproved and the TVA's reputation was reestablished.

From 1938 to 1939, Biddle served as a director and deputy chairman of the Federal Reserve Bank, until Roosevelt appointed him to be a judge on the Third Circuit Court of Appeals in Philadelphia. Bored by being

After serving as a Republican president (1901-1909), Theodore Roosevelt formed the Progressive Party in 1912 to run against the more conservative Republican candidate, William Howard Taft. Among the Progressive Party's aims were granting women the right to vote, exposing government corruption, and instituting an eight-hour workday. Roosevelt lost the election, but he split the Republican vote enough that Taft was defeated by Democrat Woodrow Wilson.

counsel: a lawyer giving legal advice or conducting a case in court

The Tennessee Valley Authority (TVA) was an independent U.S. government agency created in 1933 to provide for the complete development of the Tennessee River basin, including dams, reservoirs, hydroelectric plants, and flood control. To this day, the TVA is one of the most successful programs of the Franklin Roosevelt administration.

a judge, he was more than happy to give up the job when Roosevelt offered him the position of solicitor general in 1940. Biddle enjoyed being back in the courtroom as solicitor general, the lawyer who represents the United States government in cases before the Supreme Court. He argued and won all 15 cases he took on, including suits dealing with the regulation of interstate commerce, wages and hours, and the licensing and control of waterpower.

When the Immigration and Naturalization Service was transferred from the Department of Labor to the Department of Justice in 1940, Attorney General Robert Jackson asked Biddle to take charge of the transfer. In addition to overseeing the absorption of 4,000 new employees into the Justice Department, Biddle had to meet a new requirement by Congress that ordered the registration and fingerprinting of three and a half million aliens living in the United States. World War II had been raging in Europe

As Robert Jackson (left) looked on, Biddle was sworn in as solicitor general by Supreme Court Justice Felix Frankfurter (right) on January 22, 1940.

since 1939, and Americans were suspicious of immigrants who tried to escape the Nazis by coming to the U.S. Although the U.S. had not yet entered the war, people worried that there might be enemy spies in their midst. In an effort to relieve fear and minimize prejudice against immigrants, Biddle made speeches throughout the country and on the radio. He emphasized the important contributions foreigners had made to America and advocated equal treatment of loyal non-citizens.

In 1941, President Roosevelt turned to Francis Biddle to be the new attorney general when Robert Jackson was appointed to the Supreme Court to fill the vacancy left by the retirement of Justice Oliver Wendell Holmes. Three months after Biddle was officially sworn in, the Japanese attacked Pearl Harbor and United States declared war on Japan, Germany, and Italy. During Biddle's nearly four years in office, his single most important, all-encompassing

Franklin Delano Roosevelt (1882-1945) led the U.S. through both the Great Depression and World War II, becoming the only president to be reelected three times.

"**H**ere, I felt, would be a test of American democracy, an opportunity to show that we believed what we said. We must give [immigrants] shelter, but more than shelter. We must show a frightened world that we could share our country with the exiled and the oppressed, as we had done before."
—Francis Biddle

Robert Jackson: Supporting Roosevelt

Francis Biddle knew he had to tread carefully as Franklin D. Roosevelt's attorney general. He had seen his predecessor, Robert H. Jackson, forced to make difficult decisions about the relationship between law and political policy. In 1940, Europe was at war, France had fallen to the Nazis, and Great Britain stood alone against the German onslaught led by Adolf Hitler. The United States had proclaimed its neutrality in 1939, and isolationism was at its height in America. President Roosevelt, however, believed that it was important to U.S. national security to aid Britain in the war effort against Germany. Despite U.S. neutrality, Roosevelt decided to use his executive power to give the British 50 naval destroyers. In return, Britain gave the U.S. long-term leases on military bases in British territory in the Atlantic Ocean.

Bypassing the Senate, Roosevelt asked Jackson for an official opinion about the president's legal authority to trade the destroyers for bases. Jackson declared that the president had the power to transfer the title and possession of the destroyers, despite the fact that Britain was at war and the U.S. was a neutral nation. Jackson advised Roosevelt that he could conclude the arrangement as an executive agreement and need not present it to the Senate for a vote.

Jackson's opinion was a controversial one in 1940. Some scholars believed that exchanging the old destroyers for bases was a violation of America's neutral status. Others asserted that Jackson had used the law to conform to the president's wishes. But what if Jackson's opinion had invalidated the agreement with Britain? Would he have continued in Roosevelt's cabinet as attorney general, or would he have been replaced by someone more willing to accommodate presidential policy? Is the attorney general's role to find a legal basis for the president's actions, or to interpret the law and advise the chief executive without political consideration? It was a dilemma Biddle would also face.

consideration would be what he called "the successful prosecution of the war."

In the Cabinet

Immediately after the United States entered World War II, Biddle issued warrants for the arrest and internment of the most dangerous enemy aliens inside the country. He also instituted regulations that forbade enemy aliens from possessing weapons, did not allow them to travel outside the cities in which they lived, and banned them from military and industrial installations, airports, or docks. Biddle stated he was "determined to avoid mass internment" of enemy aliens "and the persecution of aliens that had characterized the First World War." He set up parole boards throughout the nation where aliens could have fair, impartial hearings. About 16,000 Japanese, Germans, and Italians were arrested. Only about one-third were interned; the rest were paroled, released, or sent back to their native countries. Half of those interned were Germans, and most were released within the year. Many enemy aliens who proved their loyalty to the United States, such as those serving in the armed forces, were naturalized as citizens.

internment: the confinement, especially during wartime, of a group of people

For several weeks after Pearl Harbor, selective internment by the Justice Department and the FBI was the main policy of the government. But soon officials, organizations, and newspapers in California were pressing for the evacuation of all Japanese from the West Coast. About 93,000 Japanese lived in California alone, and their presence was believed to be a grave security threat. Japanese in the U.S. were categorized into two groups: the Issei (those born in Japan who had immigrated to America) and the Nisei (second-generation Japanese who had been born in the United States). The evacuation and internment of Issei was legal, but the Nisei were American citizens who had the same constitutional rights that Biddle or any other member of the cabinet did. Californians and their leaders, however, questioned the loyalty and allegiance of all

naturalize: to grant full citizenship to someone of foreign birth

Japanese. Governor Culbert Olson, California Attorney General Earl Warren, and Mayor Fletcher Bowron of Los Angeles all supported mass internment. They were indifferent to the fact that this would deprive about 80,000 American citizens (Nisei) of their civil rights.

The suspicion, fear, and hatred against the Japanese did not extend to German or Italian Americans. Racism was probably the reason for the different attitudes. The Japanese looked different than Europeans and didn't always blend into American society as easily as most Germans and Italians did. They often lived together in their own areas and practiced their own traditions. Many had done

Propaganda posters like this one, which fueled hatred of Japanese enemy soldiers, also helped inspire prejudice against Japanese Americans.

well as farmers and businesspeople, and their white neighbors were envious of their achievements. Prejudice against the Japanese was certainly not new. Since 1798, federal law had barred all Asian immigrants from becoming U.S. citizens, and the Oriental Exclusion Act of 1924 had banned further immigration from Japan. In California, the Alien Land Act of 1913 prohibited Japanese from owning land.

The Roberts Commission Report on Pearl Harbor, released in January 1942, noted that there had been espionage activities by the Japanese in Hawaii before the December attack. Although there had been no instances of sabotage or espionage in California, this report was used as a reason to go ahead with internment. Francis Biddle, however, strongly opposed evacuating Japanese American citizens. "I thought at the time that the program was ill-advised . . . and unnecessarily cruel, taking Japanese who were not suspect, and Japanese Americans whose rights were disregarded, from their homes and from their businesses to sit idly in the lonely misery of barracks while the war was being fought in the world beyond," he later wrote.

Biddle was attacked in the press for his opposition to internment. Many people felt that a concern for individual rights could not be allowed to interfere with national security during wartime. Biddle, in fact, was the only high-level government official to protest action against Japanese Americans. He wrote to Secretary of War Henry Stimson that "the Department of Justice would not under any circumstances evacuate American citizens." Biddle said that if the military was intent on such a policy, it could only be accomplished legally if the area and action were considered militarily essential. He also expressed his opinion to Franklin Roosevelt, "but the decision had been made by the president," he wrote. "It was, he said, a matter of military judgment. I did not think I should oppose it any further. The Department of Justice, as I had made it clear to him from the beginning, was opposed to and would have nothing to do with the evacuation."

espionage: the use of spies by governments, corporations, or organizations to discover military, political, technical, or personal secrets

"Such a program was expensive and troublesome. It diverted large numbers of Army personnel from the more immediate job of getting on with the war, and thousands of civilian workers, particularly Japanese farmers, were rendered idle. It subjected Americans to the shame of being classed as enemies of their native country without any evidence indicating disloyalty. American citizens of Japanese origin were not even handled like aliens of the other enemy nationalities . . . but as untouchables, a group who could not be trusted and had to be shut up only because they were of Japanese descent."
—Francis Biddle

On February 19, 1942, Roosevelt signed Executive Order 9066, authorizing the army to establish military areas from which any civilian could be excluded. Western Oregon and Washington, the southern half of Arizona, and the entire state of California were all designated as military areas. Although the order did not mention the Japanese specifically, it effectively allowed the U.S. government to remove all people of Japanese descent from the Pacific coast and transport them to inland areas. Italian and German aliens were not to be removed.

The largest group migration in American history began on March 22, 1942. More than 110,000 Japanese were transported to 15 temporary assembly centers and then

As his young son looks on, a Japanese American merchant posts a sign on his store advertising a sale before his evacuation from San Francisco.

moved to 10 permanent relocation camps in Utah, Arizona, Colorado, Wyoming, Arkansas, California, and Idaho. With little time to sell or rent their homes, businesses, or possessions, the Japanese lost nearly everything they owned. They could take only what they could carry with them, and many sold their belongings to white neighbors at minimal prices. The conditions in the camps were harsh: families lived crowded together in bare, flimsy, hastily built barracks, surrounded by barbed wire and armed guards. Located in remote areas, the camps were unbearably hot in the summer and freezing in the winter. Schools and med-ical services could be rare, and the food was poor. Some

The internment camp at Tule Lake, California. Set aside for Japanese judged "dis-loyal" to the United States, it was the site of demonstra-tions, strikes, and occasionally violence.

Executive Order 9066 in the Supreme Court

Three major Supreme Court cases tested the constitutionality of the government's treatment of Japanese American citizens during World War II. As a later Chief Justice, William Rehnquist, described them, these lawsuits claimed that internment "was unconstitutional because it proceeded on the basis that this entire racial group was disloyal rather than being based on any individual determinations of disloyalty."

Gordon Hirabayashi, a Nisei born to Issei parents in Seattle, was a college student at the University of Washington. He disobeyed a military curfew requirement, did not register for evacuation, and was subsequently arrested. He was indicted and convicted in a federal court, and his case progressed to the Supreme Court, where he claimed that the laws he was accused of violating were unconstitutional. In *Hirabayashi v. United States* (1943), the Supreme Court ruled only on the question of the curfew requirement, not on the internment question. Chief Justice Harlan Stone upheld the constitutionality of the curfew, stating, "Whatever views we may entertain regarding the loyalty to this country of the citizens of Japanese ancestry, we cannot reject as unfounded the judgment of the military authorities and of Congress that there were disloyal members of that population, whose number and strength could not be precisely and quickly ascertained."

Fred Korematsu, another young Nisei born to Issei parents in America, refused to evacuate the West Coast when ordered to do so. Instead, he remained in San Leandro, California, and was arrested for violating a military exclusion order. In *Korematsu v. United States* (1944), the Court ruled on whether loyal Japanese citizens could be removed from their homes and relocated to detention camps because of their ancestry. A majority of the Court upheld the exclusion and relocation of Japanese Americans, stating that the government had acted constitutionally. Justice Hugo Black, writing for the Court, said, "Korematsu was not excluded from the Military Area because of hostility to him or his race. He *was* excluded because we are at war with the Japanese Empire, because the properly constituted military authorities feared an invasion of our West Coast and felt constrained to take proper security measures, because they decided that the military urgency of the situation demanded that all citizens of Japanese ancestry be segregated from the West Coast temporarily." In a dissenting opinion, Justice Frank Murphy declared that the evacuation legalized racism.

Mitsuye Endo, a U.S. citizen of Japanese ancestry, had submitted to relocation and was in an internment camp in Utah. She filed a petition for a writ of habeas corpus, claiming that as a loyal citizen with no charges against her, she was entitled to be given her

Liberal Justices Hugo Black (1886-1971) and Frank Murphy (1890-1949, bottom) disagreed on the legality of Japanese internment.

freedom and allowed to leave the camp. In *Ex Parte Endo* (1944), the Supreme Court ruled that Executive Order 9066 confirmed the evacuation of Japanese Americans from military zones, but did not specifically mention detention after the evacuation. Since the government agreed that Endo was a loyal citizen and there were no charges against her, the Court ruled that she was entitled to be released from the camp.

In 1980, the U.S. Congress established the Commission on Wartime Relocation and Internment of Civilians (CWRIC) to reevaluate Executive Order 9066. In 1983, the committee issued a report that concluded, "Executive Order 9066 was not justified by military necessity, and the decisions that followed from it—exclusion, detention . . . were not founded upon military considerations. The broad historical causes that shaped these decisions were race prejudice, war hysteria, and a failure of political leadership." As a result, teams of lawyers brought a series of actions against the government, successfully overturning the convictions of Gordon Hirabayashi, Fred Korematsu, and a third Nisei, Minoru Yasui, who had also challenged the order.

★ ★

internees were beaten or even shot by guards if they tried to escape or "caused trouble."

Throughout the remainder of World War II, Biddle advocated releasing Japanese Americans from the internment camps—especially after the tide had turned in America's favor in the war and there was no longer any threat of a Japanese invasion on the West Coast. On December 30, 1943, Biddle wrote to Roosevelt, "The present procedure of keeping loyal American citizens in concentration camps on the basis of race for longer than is absolutely necessary is dangerous and repugnant to the principles of our government. It is also necessary to act now so that the agitation against these citizens does not continue after the war." Despite Biddle's protests, the Japanese were not released from internment camps until the war's end in 1945.

saboteur: a person who commits sabotage, the deliberate damage of equipment or property to undermine a government or military operation

In addition to being involved in the controversy surrounding the evacuation and internment of Japanese Americans, Biddle was an important participant in a high-profile wartime case involving Nazi saboteurs apprehended on American soil. Four Germans landed on a Long Island, New York, beach on the night of June 13, 1942, and four others came ashore at Ponte Vedra Beach near Jacksonville, Florida, on June 17. They carried a variety of explosives, a large amount of cash, and detailed plans of key American railroad centers, bridges, electric plants, and industries. The authorities apprehended all of the Germans within 10 days.

President Roosevelt informed Biddle that he strongly favored a trial by court-martial and the death sentence for all the men. The attorney general was faced with a legal dilemma. The men had not yet committed any acts of sabotage when they were arrested, though their intent was perfectly clear. Under civil law, Biddle believed he would not have a strong enough case for attempted sabotage. A federal law covering conspiracies to commit crimes did apply, but the penalty was three years of imprisonment. A death sentence could be sought only if the men were tried by a military court, and Biddle knew the right of the government to hold such a court-martial would eventually have to be decided in the Supreme Court.

President Roosevelt signed an executive order that set up a special military commission, consisting of seven officers, to try the eight saboteurs for "offenses against the law of war and the Articles of War." Votes from two-thirds of the commission members were needed for a conviction and a death sentence. No reporters were permitted at the trial and there were no press releases or announcements. Biddle was the chief prosecutor for the government. Two

conviction: a judgment by a jury or judge that a person is guilty of a crime as charged

Biddle questions an FBI agent during the third day of the Nazi saboteur trial

appeal: a request made after a trial, asking a higher court (usually a court of appeals) to reverse or set aside the decision made at the trial level

of the eight Germans cooperated with the U.S. authorities and testified against the others. They then filed petitions for habeas corpus in federal court. Their requests cited the *Ex Parte Milligan* case of 1866, in which the Court held that even in a time of war, civilians could not be tried by a military court as long as the civil courts were still open and functioning and martial law had not been declared. The petitions were denied by the district court and appealed to the Supreme Court, where Biddle argued that *Milligan* was not a "binding precedent" (a legal decision that must be followed in later, similar cases) and did not apply to a situation involving the law of war.

On July 31, 1942, the Supreme Court affirmed the decision of the district court, denying the Germans' petitions for habeas corpus. As Biddle later summarized the Court's position, "spies and enemy combatants without uniform, coming secretly through the lines to wage war by destruction of life and property, were, by universal agreement, not entitled to the status of prisoners of war, but were offenders against the law of war, and subject to trial and punishment by military tribunals." All eight saboteurs were found guilty on August 1 and sentenced to death on August 3. For the two men who had cooperated with the government, Biddle recommended long prison sentences instead. Roosevelt accepted Biddle's recommendation, and on August 8, six of the Germans were executed at the district jail. In 1948, after the war was over, President Harry Truman cut short the prison terms of the two remaining saboteurs and they were both sent back to Germany.

It had taken only six weeks to arrest the saboteurs, try them, and carry out their sentences. Biddle declared, "The defendants had been given every right afforded by our law . . . by the country to which they had come in order to wreck war plants. It was an extraordinary example of justice at its best, prompt, yet fair—in striking contrast to what was going on in Germany."

President Franklin Roosevelt died on April 12, 1945. At the request of the new president, Harry S. Truman, Biddle resigned as attorney general in June 1945.

Looking Forward

Within months after resigning from the cabinet, Biddle was appointed by Truman to be the American member of the International Military Tribunal at Nuremberg, Germany. This tribunal tried Nazi leaders for war crimes and crimes against humanity. Six million Jewish people and five million gypsies, Slavs, Poles, homosexuals, political prisoners, mentally deficient people, and others had been

Biddle as a judge at the Nuremberg trials. Next to him sits the alternate American judge, John J. Parker.

murdered by the Nazis. The Nuremberg trial revealed these atrocities to the world through testimony, film, and documents. Of the 21 Germans tried, 11 were sentenced to death, 7 were sent to prison, and 3 were acquitted. Biddle believed that the tribunal's most important declaration was that individuals and not just governments must be held responsible for war crimes. "In making responsibility an individual matter," wrote Biddle, "the tribunal rejected the fiction of national irresponsibility."

From 1950 to 1953, Biddle chaired Americans for Democratic Action, an organization that promoted liberal causes. In 1951 he wrote a book called *The Fear of Freedom*, which criticized oppressive measures taken by the government to find and punish communists and other "subversives." Biddle argued against censorsing textbooks, requiring educators to take loyalty oaths, "guilt by association" (labeling people as communists without proof because they associated with communists), and the tactics of the House Committee on Un-American Activities. Later, he would also oppose the anti-Communist hysteria generated by Senator Joseph McCarthy. In 1955, Biddle headed a committee to plan Franklin D. Roosevelt's memorial.

Reflecting on his tenure as attorney general years later, Biddle regretted the internment of Japanese Americans. He wondered whether things would have been different if Secretary of War Stimson had opposed the action or if he had urged Stimson to resist the president. "If Stimson had stood firm . . . the president would have followed his advice," wrote Biddle in his autobiography. "And if . . . I had urged the secretary to resist the pressure of his subordinates, the result might have been different. But I was . . . disinclined to insist on my view to an elder statesman whose wisdom and integrity I greatly respected."

No Japanese American was ever tried for treason, espionage, or sabotage in World War II. In 1976, President Gerald Ford formally revoked Executive Order 9066 and praised the contributions of Japanese Americans to their nation. In 1988, President Ronald Reagan signed a bill that publicly apologized for the evacuation and internment of Japanese Americans during the war, and the government gave survivors a tax-free payment of $20,000 each

Francis Biddle died in Massachusetts on October 4, 1968, at the age of 82. He had been an attorney general who supported his president, but he also followed his own moral principles by opposing presidential policy toward Japanese Americans. In attempting to satisfy the dual issues of loyalty and conscience, Biddle was criticized by both sides. In hindsight, however, he wished he had done more on the side of conscience.

President Ronald Reagan signed the bill authorizing reparations payments to survivors of the internment camps on August 10, 1988.

★ ★ 5 ★ ★

HERBERT BROWNELL

Beginning the Fight for Equality

Herbert Brownell's first visit to Washington, D.C., was in the summer of 1924. The 20-year-old had received a scholarship to Yale Law School. He and his brother Samuel, a graduate student at Yale, were on their way to the campus in New Haven, Connecticut, for the fall term. The two brothers had driven from their home in Nebraska in a used Model T Ford and decided to do some sightseeing in the nation's capital before settling into academic life. After finding a cheap hotel near Union Station for a dollar a night, the Brownells headed over to the White House like any other tourists. It happened to be Armed Services Preparedness Day, and a parade was scheduled. President Calvin Coolidge and his cabinet were expected to attend, so Brownell and his brother staked out a spot opposite the reviewing stand on the parade route. Several hours later, the dignitaries arrived and the procession began.

"I recall in particular . . . the presence of Coolidge's attorney general," wrote Brownell in his memoirs nearly 70 years later. "[He] was seated almost directly opposite from where I stood." That man was Harlan Fiske Stone, who had helped to restore confidence and credibility to the Department of Justice after the Teapot Dome oil reserve scandals of the Warren Harding administration. "Little did I realize," declared Brownell, "that one day I would occupy the great office that he then held." Brownell had another

By supporting desegregation during the 1950s, the 62nd attorney general, Herbert Brownell (1904-1996), demonstrated the positive effect his office could have on civil rights.

Harlan Fiske Stone (1872-1946) helped the government recover from the Teapot Dome scandal, in which Secretary of the Interior Albert B. Fall accepted bribes from oilman Harry Sinclair in exchange for secretly leasing oil reserves in Teapot Dome, Wyoming, to Sinclair's company. (Fall was convicted of the crime and sentenced to a year in prison.) After serving as attorney general, Stone went on to become a justice (and later chief justice) of the Supreme Court.

link to the position of attorney general. His great-uncle, William H. H. Miller, had served in the post from 1889 to 1893 under President Benjamin Harrison. Sixty years later, in 1953, Herbert Brownell was confirmed as the 62nd attorney general, under President Dwight D. Eisenhower. One of the first things Brownell did was to hang an official portrait of his great-uncle in his office and place nearby a bound volume of his ancestor's published opinions.

Brownell faced many controversial issues in the 1950s as Eisenhower's chief law-enforcement officer, but he was remembered most for his pivotal role in the area of civil rights. He used his position as attorney general to enforce the Supreme Court's desegregation decision in *Brown v. Board of Education* and to persuade a reluctant chief executive to support the first significant civil rights legislation passed by Congress since the decade after the Civil War.

The Formative Years

Born on February 20, 1904, Herbert Brownell was one of seven children of Herbert and May Brownell. His parents were originally from upstate New York, but they had relocated in 1891 when Herbert Sr. was offered a position as science professor at a teacher's college in Peru, Nebraska. The family moved to Lincoln in 1910, after Herbert Sr. accepted a professorship at the University of Nebraska, and all seven children attended college there. Reading, music, and current events were often discussed in the Brownell household, and Herbert Jr. became interested in politics at an early age.

Brownell lived at home while attending the University of Nebraska, where he earned a B.A. degree in 1924. At Yale Law School, Brownell excelled in constitutional law and was editor-in-chief of the *Yale Law Journal*. After graduation in 1927, he was admitted to the New York bar and began working for the firm of Root, Clark, Buckner, Howland & Ballantine in New York City. Two years later,

Brownell accepted a position at the smaller firm of Lord, Day & Lord, where he practiced corporate-securities law.

Brownell was a moderate Republican who believed in social reform and opposed the high government spending of Franklin D. Roosevelt's administration. After several years as an attorney in New York, he joined the Young Republicans and in 1931 became a candidate for the New York State Assembly. His campaign manager was Thomas Dewey, who would prove to be an important ally. Brownell ran for office from Manhattan's Tenth Assembly District, which included Democratic areas such as Greenwich Village, Times Square, and Gramercy Park. He narrowly lost the election, but he did meet the woman he eventually married, Doris McCarter. They would later have four children together.

Assembly terms were only one year long, so Brownell ran again the following year and won by 300 votes. "My entry into the assembly—the first of five terms—was news-worthy . . . because I was one of only a very few Republicans statewide to defeat an incumbent Democrat in the 1932 Roosevelt landslide," he declared. As an elected representative, Brownell learned much about the give and take of legislative politics and made important contacts with both Republicans and Democrats throughout the state. He sponsored legislation dealing with child labor, organized crime, parks improvement, the economy, public schools, and social welfare. Brownell also worked again with Thomas Dewey, who was now the special prosecutor of organized crime in New York State.

By the end of his fifth term in 1937, Brownell decided not to run for reelection. Almost immediately, he was appointed general counsel for the upcoming 1939-1940 World's Fair to be held in New York City. Brownell held this position for three years. When the fair ended, he became campaign manager for Edgar Nathan Jr., who was elected borough president of Manhattan in 1941. Thomas Dewey then asked Brownell to manage his New York state

This political cartoon poked fun at Brownell while he was chairman of the Republican National Committee in 1944. It portrayed him and Democratic National Committee Chairman Robert Hannegan pointing happily at a large bag of voter registrations. Both party leaders claimed that the high number of registered voters would give them an advantage in the upcoming election.

gubernatorial campaign in 1942. With Brownell's help, Dewey won a decisive victory, and as governor of New York, he became a national leader of the Republican Party.

In the decade between 1942 and 1952, the experienced Brownell managed Republican campaigns at the highest level. Dewey set his sights on the presidency, and Brownell turned his skills and attention to building a political base and gaining national support. Brownell was appointed chairman of the Republican National Committee while managing Dewey's presidential campaign in 1944. Although Franklin Roosevelt was reelected president, Dewey received more than 22 million votes nationwide, doing better than any of Roosevelt's three previous

Republican challengers. In 1948, Brownell became campaign manager for Dewey's second presidential bid, this time against Harry S. Truman, Roosevelt's successor. Dewey was a big favorite to win the election, but he was upset by Truman after the Republicans lost the farm vote. Some Dewey supporters had been so confident of a Republican victory that they hadn't even bothered to vote.

When General Dwight D. Eisenhower, Supreme Commander of the Allied forces in World War II and now the first head of the North Atlantic Treaty Organization (NATO), decided to run for president in 1952 as a moderate Republican, he turned to Herbert Brownell to manage his political campaign. With Brownell's help, Eisenhower won the Republican nomination away from conservative senator Robert Taft of Ohio, then defeated Democratic candidate Adlai Stevenson of Illinois in the 1952 election. It was a landslide victory, and Eisenhower offered Brownell the position of chief of staff in his administration.

The North Atlantic Treaty Organization (NATO) was established in 1949 to counter threats of aggression by the Soviet Union and safeguard the countries of Europe and North America.

"You know I'm a lawyer," explained Brownell to the newly elected president, "and I have a deep interest in the law. I've spent twenty-five years at the bar and want to spend another twenty-five there." Eisenhower replied, "So you want to remain a lawyer. . . . Well, how about being attorney general?" After consulting with his wife, Brownell accepted the offer. He resigned from his law firm, disposed of his investments, and moved his family to the nation's capital. Before he left Washington five years later, some people would call him the conscience of the Eisenhower administration.

In the Cabinet

Upon taking office, Attorney General Brownell was immediately involved in a landmark decision by the U.S. Supreme Court that changed the civil rights movement for all time. *Brown v. Board of Education* was a combination of five similar cases brought against segregated school districts by black parents throughout the nation. The case was

Dwight David Eisenhower (1890-1969), nicknamed "Ike," easily swept to victory in the 1952 election after winning popularity as a World War II hero. He concentrated on foreign policy (such as stopping the spread of communism) during his two terms in office, but civil rights would also become a pressing issue.

The National Association for the Advancement of Colored People (NAACP) was formed in 1910 with the goal of ending racial discrimination and segregation through lawsuits and nonviolent protests.

pending: not yet decided; awaiting a trial or settlement

named for Linda Brown, a black third-grader in Topeka, Kansas, who had to walk six blocks and then catch a bus to get to the black elementary school, when the white school was much nearer her home. In addition, the black school was in poorer condition, understaffed, and underfunded. When Linda's father tried to enroll her at the white school, she was denied admission because she was black. With the help of the National Association for the Advancement of Colored People (NAACP), the Browns and other families went to court in an attempt to overturn *Plessy v. Ferguson* (1896), a case that legitimized separate public facilities for blacks and whites. Their case went to the Supreme Court in December 1952 and was still pending when Eisenhower became president.

Plessy v. Ferguson: Separate But Equal

During and after the Civil War, three amendments were made to the Constitution in an effort to provide freedom and equality for African Americans. In 1865, the 13th Amendment abolished slavery. In 1868, the 14th Amendment declared equal protection under the law: Confederate states were required to ratify the amendment in order to be readmitted to the Union. In 1870, the 15th Amendment granted equal voting rights. The equality promised by these amendments was not realized, however. Throughout the South, "Jim Crow" laws were passed to restrict blacks' legal rights and institute racial segregation in all public facilities. (Jim Crow was the name of a character in a popular song of the time.)

The legitimacy of these laws came into question in 1896, in the Supreme Court case *Plessy v. Ferguson*. A black man, Homer Adolph Plessy, had been arrested in 1892 for refusing to move out of his seat in a whites-only railroad car in Louisiana. Plessy was convicted by Judge John H. Ferguson of breaking the state segregation law. Plessy appealed his conviction, claiming that separating the races on train cars violated the 14th Amendment's statement that "No State shall make or enforce any law which shall abridge the privileges or immunities of citizens of the United States; nor shall any State deprive any person of life, liberty, or property, without due process of law; nor deny to any person within its jurisdiction the equal protection of the laws."

When the case reached the Supreme Court, the majority of justices upheld the local statute allowing racially segregated but supposedly equal railroad cars. The Court stated that racial separation did not make or imply inferiority of one race over the other. It also declared that the object of the 14th Amendment was political, not social, equality; therefore, it allowed for racial segregation. This decision sanctioned Jim Crow laws, giving a legal basis for segregation of blacks and whites not only in railroad cars, but also in all other areas of society, including schools, restaurants, and hotels. "Separate but equal" became an accepted legal doctrine, especially in the South, for more than half a century.

Only Justice John Harlan dissented in *Plessy v. Ferguson*, believing that the Louisiana statute was unconstitutional. He wrote, "In view of the Constitution, in the eye of the law, there is in this country no superior, dominant, ruling class of citizens. . . . Our Constitution is color-blind, and neither knows nor tolerates classes among citizens. In respect of civil rights, all citizens are equal before the law."

Linda Brown

The Supreme Court did not reach a decision on *Brown* by the end of its term in June 1953, but instead set the case for reargument in October. The Court invited Attorney General Brownell to file a brief and appear as an amicus curiae (friend of court). Initially, Eisenhower felt the government should decline the Court's request. Brownell, however, convinced the chief executive that a refusal would strain relations with the Court. Brownell emphasized his duty to the law and the Constitution, and Eisenhower deferred to his attorney general.

Brownell and his deputies prepared a detailed written brief on *Brown*. But when it came time to state the administration's policies on segregation in schools, Eisenhower did not want to take a stand because, as Brownell put it, "he feared interfering with the workings of the judicial branch." Brownell convinced Eisenhower that the administration should state its views. Again, Eisenhower deferred to the attorney general, and Brownell's position that public school segregation was unconstitutional—that "separate was inherently unequal"—became that of the administration.

In a unanimous decision issued on May 17, 1954, the Supreme Court struck down the separate but equal doctrine of *Plessy*, declaring racial segregation in the public schools to be unconstitutional because it violated the equal protection clause of the 14th Amendment. As Justice Earl Warren wrote in his opinion, "To separate [black students] from others of similar age and qualifications solely because of their race generates a feeling of inferiority as to their status in the community that may affect their hearts and minds in a way unlikely ever to be undone." The decision on how to enforce the ruling was postponed, however, until the Court met again in 1955.

Brownell and his staff prepared another brief and argument for *Brown II*. They recommended that each school district submit a desegregation plan to the local federal district court for approval within 90 days. The Supreme Court adopted Brownell's suggestion, but it did not set a

Three of the attorneys who helped win Brown v. Board of Education *congratulate one another after the Supreme Court's decision: (left to right) George E. C. Hayes, Thurgood Marshall, and James M. Nabrit. As chief counsel of the NAACP's Legal Defense and Educational Fund, Marshall directed the team's strategy in the case. He later went on to become the first African American justice of the Supreme Court.*

timetable. Instead, the Court ruled that desegregation was to take place "with all deliberate speed," which was interpreted by some Southern officials as an opportunity to delay. Brownell criticized the Court for not setting a schedule that allowed the decision to be properly enforced.

After the *Brown II* decision, 100 members of Congress signed a statement called the Southern Manifesto that pledged their complete opposition and resistance to desegregation in the public schools. Other people expressed their hatred of desegregation by burning crosses on Supreme Court justices' lawns, and an intruder dumped kerosene on the ground outside Brownell's house. When local school board officials tried to comply with *Brown*, rioting occurred in some areas. The Justice Department,

One especially vocal opponent of desegregation was Arkansas governor Orval Faubus (1910-1994).

however, could not intervene with school boards or state officials directly. It could help with enforcement only if the local school boards involved the federal courts.

In 1957, in Little Rock, Arkansas, opposition to the *Brown* decision came from a group of white parents who asked Governor Orval Faubus to intervene after a federal judge ordered desegregation of the local high school. Faubus ignored the federal court order and used the state national guard to prevent nine black students from attending white Central High School. Large crowds began to assemble in Little Rock, and only the presence of the guardsmen prevented mob violence from erupting against the black children trying to enter the school. Then the governor went on television throughout the state to announce he was removing the National Guard. Fearing a disaster, the mayor of Little Rock asked for federal help in keeping order. Eisenhower consulted his attorney general, who advised him that he had the power to enforce the law. "When state officers refuse or fail to discharge their duty . . . it becomes the responsibility of the national government, through the chief executive, to dispel any such forcible resistance to federal law. Otherwise, lawlessness would be permitted to exist for lack of any counteracting force," wrote Brownell in his official opinion.

As a result, Eisenhower ordered the 101st Airborne Division to Little Rock and brought the Arkansas National Guard under federal control. Then he addressed the nation on television to explain his actions and the situation in Little Rock. The nine black students entered the high school safely, beginning the desegregation process. Later,

The "Little Rock Nine," as the black students were known, had to be escorted in and out of Central High School by soldiers for weeks. They endured intimidation and violence from their white classmates and continuing opposition from the community. In 1958, Orval Faubus closed Little Rock high schools to avoid further integration. They reopened in 1959, but the full integration of all levels of Little Rock's public school system was not achieved until 1972.

the Supreme Court unanimously upheld the constitutionality of the president's actions in Arkansas. "Eisenhower's intervention," declared Brownell, "dramatically showed that the federal government was supreme in enforcing the Constitution."

In addition to helping desegregate the South, Brownell became the driving force behind the passage of the first federal civil rights legislation since 1875. In 1956, with the unenthusiastic support of President Eisenhower and his cabinet, Brownell directed the Justice Department's civil rights specialists to draft a bill that would give the attorney general and the Justice Department direct power of enforcement when civil rights violations occurred. The draft consisted of four specific proposals: 1) the creation of a bipartisan civil rights commission, appointed by the president, that would hold hearings and recommend new civil rights legislation; 2) the formation of a new civil rights division within the Justice Department and an assistant attorney general to head it; 3) additional power to the attorney general to "seek injunctive relief against the obstruction of civil rights" through civil suits; and 4) "establishment of enforcement machinery . . . to guarantee the right to vote in federal elections for black citizens."

The objections to part three of Brownell's civil rights bill were summed up by Senator Sam Ervin of North Carolina, who called it "deliberately designed to vest in the attorney general the autocratic and despotic power to nullify state laws [and] to institute and prosecute at public expense lawsuits as numberless as the sand for the avowed benefit of any alien, citizen, or private corporation."

President Eisenhower distanced himself from Brownell's bill, requesting that it be sent to Congress as a Department of Justice proposal, not a White House proposal. He also did not agree with part three, which expanded the attorney general's enforcement powers, and he ordered that it be removed before the legislation was sent to Congress. In a prior arrangement with Brownell, however, Congressman Kenneth Keating of the House Judiciary Committee purposely asked to see the section that had been deleted. By doing so, Keating could include it in the final bill, which was passed by the House on July 23. The bill then went to the Senate, where it remained in the Judiciary Committee for the rest of the 1956 session. Brownell called the Judiciary Committee "the traditional graveyard of civil rights legislation," because it had prevented most previously proposed bills from ever reaching the Senate floor. To make matters worse, the Judiciary Committee was currently headed by a prosegregation senator from Mississippi.

During Eisenhower's 1956 reelection campaign, he publicly endorsed all four parts of the Civil Rights Act, although privately he still opposed part three. After Eisenhower was reelected and the Civil Rights Act was resubmitted in the 1957 session, Brownell enlisted the help of Vice President Richard Nixon and Republican senator William Knowland of California to get the bill before the full Senate. Southern senators fought the legislation, especially the controversial part three. Brownell wanted a debate on the Senate floor, but Eisenhower chose the way of compromise. He agreed to drop section three to get the remaining provisions passed.

President Eisenhower signed the Civil Rights Act into law on September 9, 1957.

Historians differ about the roles of Brownell and Eisenhower in passing the Civil Rights Act of 1957. Some believe that Brownell jeopardized his own position to get the bill introduced in Congress and may have overstepped his authority as a member of the cabinet. Others believe that Eisenhower's strategy was to let Brownell take the lead all along. Historian Richard Kluger, however, gave Brownell the credit: "The act owed its existence not to the president, whose ineptness nearly submarined it, but to his attorney general, Herbert Brownell, one of the very few pro-civil-rights people in the Eisenhower high command."

Brownell continued to support civil rights as attorney general, consistently encouraging Eisenhower to appoint federal judges in the South who were sensitive to civil rights issues and independent enough to carry out desegregation. Brownell believed advancing the cause of civil rights was "not simply a matter of personal prejudice or policy view, it was a matter of constitutional duty," and he obtained the president's support slowly "each step of the way." Brownell declared, "Before I left office, everything had been done that legally could be done to establish *Brown v. Board of Education* as the law of the land."

Civil rights issues dominated Brownell's tenure as attorney general, but he also played a significant role in drafting the 25th Amendment to the Constitution and promoting its adoption. Written as a result of President Eisenhower's heart attack in 1955, the amendment made provisions for a situation in which the president was disabled in any way and could not do his job. Brownell and his staff developed the substance of the amendment, although it was not passed by Congress until 1965 and not completely ratified by the states until February 10, 1967—after the assassination of President John F. Kennedy had made the issue more pressing.

Brownell left the cabinet at the end of 1957 to return to his private law practice in New York City. His many accomplishments in civil rights made him an unpopular man in the South, where one newspaper editorial stated, "No tears are being shed for the retirement of Herbert Brownell, Jr., as attorney general. The frightful mess the South, and the country, are in is probably as much his responsibility as that of any living man." Brownell, however, looked back at his achievements in civil rights as the "high points" of his years as attorney general.

Looking Forward

Brownell's departure from Washington, D.C., was not the end of his career in public service. He was chosen by various presidents to represent the United States at important events, to serve on special committees, or to give his legal opinion. He sat as an arbitrator of disputes in the local federal court and was a member of the International Court of Arbitration at The Hague in the Netherlands. After 62 years at the bar, Brownell retired from the practice of law in 1989 at the age of 85. He died on May 1, 1996, in New York City.

Reflecting back on his cabinet days, Herbert Brownell described Eisenhower as a chief executive who delegated responsibility to his cabinet members. "I liked the opportunity to turn broad policy and theories of government into solutions," Brownell wrote. "I liked the challenge to use my initiative and to be an activist in the office of attorney general." Many future attorneys general would follow that pattern, particularly in the area of civil rights.

★ ★ *6* ★ ★

ROBERT F. KENNEDY

The Struggle for Civil Rights

1968 was a tumultuous year in the United States. American involvement in the war in Vietnam was escalating, and opposition to it was growing. President Lyndon Johnson shocked the nation when he announced he would not run for reelection. In the civil rights movement, Martin Luther King Jr.'s philosophy of nonviolent resistance was being openly challenged by militant groups such as the Black Panthers. Meanwhile, Senator Robert Kennedy of New York was busy campaigning for the Democratic presidential nomination. On the night of April 4, he was scheduled to speak in a black neighborhood in Indianapolis. Kennedy was a popular figure among African Americans, who remembered the efforts that he and his brother John had made on behalf of King and the civil rights struggle in the early 1960s.

On his way to Indianapolis, Robert Kennedy learned that King had been assassinated in Memphis, Tennessee. The Indianapolis chief of police feared there would be rioting in black neighborhoods and advised Kennedy not to appear. His police escort refused to accompany him into the black ghetto, stating there was no way his safety could be guaranteed. Kennedy, however, insisted on facing the enthusiastic supporters who had gathered to hear him speak. None of them had heard the news about King. It was dark and cold as he got up on the back of a flatbed

Robert F. Kennedy (1925-1968) may be best known for his famous family and his tragic death, but he also shaped legal policy during the turbulent 1960s as the 64th U.S. attorney general.

truck to address the crowd of nearly a thousand people. Waving away his prepared speech, Kennedy spoke from some scribbled notes he had made on the airplane.

"I have bad news for you," Kennedy announced, "for all of our fellow citizens, and people who love peace all over the world, and that is that Martin Luther King was shot and killed tonight." The crowd gasped in shock and horror and shouted, "No, no." Quietly, Kennedy continued, "For those of you who are black and are tempted to be filled with hatred and distrust at the injustice of such an act, against all white people, I can only say that I feel in my own heart the same kind of feeling. I had a member of my family killed, but he was killed by a white man. . . . You can be filled with bitterness, with hatred, and a desire for revenge . . . or we can make an effort, as Martin Luther King did, to understand and to comprehend, and to replace

As a leader of the black civil rights movement, Martin Luther King Jr. (1929-1968) used nonviolent resistance, such as sit-ins and marches to challenge segregation laws in the South. He won the Nobel Peace Prize in 1964 and was murdered four years later by James Earl Ray, a racist and escaped convict. (Sentenced to 99 years in prison, Ray died there in 1998.)

that violence, that stain of bloodshed that has spread across our land . . . with compassion and love." That night and in the days that followed, there were riots in 110 American cities. Thirty-nine people were killed and over 2,500 were injured. It took more than 75,000 National Guardsmen patrolling city streets to restore order. But there was no violence in Indianapolis.

The special connection that Robert Kennedy shared with African Americans in their struggle for civil rights was obvious that night, as it was throughout his presidential campaign. But that had not always been the case. Early in Kennedy's political career, the issue of racial equality had often taken a backseat to politics and expediency. "I won't say I stayed awake nights worrying about civil rights before I became attorney general," he admitted. During his years as head of the Justice Department, Kennedy faced dramatic events and difficult decisions that were crucial in altering his views. His resulting actions made him one of the most famous, popular, and controversial attorneys general in history.

The Formative Years

Born on November 20, 1925, in Brookline, Massachusetts, Robert Francis Kennedy was the seventh of nine children of Rose Fitzgerald and Joseph Patrick Kennedy. The wealthy Kennedy family was descended from Irish immigrants who had prospered in the United States.

As a child, Robert was small, shy, and clumsy, overshadowed by his outgoing older siblings. In a family where politics and current events were discussed by all the children at the dinner table, Joseph Kennedy's attention focused mainly on his two oldest sons, Joe Jr. and John. Robert was in awe of these brothers, who both enlisted in the military when World War II broke out. Eager to prove himself, he joined the Naval Reserve as an apprentice seaman in October 1943, shortly before his 18th birthday. By the time his naval instruction was complete, however, the war was over. But Robert did serve for a time aboard the new destroyer *Joseph P. Kennedy Jr.*, named after his oldest brother, who had been killed in an airplane crash during the war.

After his discharge from the navy in 1946, Robert helped get his brother John elected to the Massachusetts House of Representatives. Robert then attended Harvard University, where he graduated 1948. He then enrolled in the University of Virginia Law School and became president of its Student Legal Forum, which brought in outside speakers. Robert Kennedy showed his first glimmer of concern for racial equality when, in the spring of 1951, he invited Dr. Ralph Bunche to address the students. Bunche was an African American diplomat who had won the Nobel Peace Prize in 1950. At that time, the University of Virginia was an all-white school, and Virginia state law prohibited blacks and whites from sitting together in an auditorium. Bunche told Kennedy that he would not appear before a segregated audience. Determined that Bunche should speak, Kennedy convinced the university president to open the lecture to everyone.

In 1950, 24-year-old Robert Kennedy married Ethel Skakel, with whom he eventually had 11 children. Upon finishing law school in 1951, he served in 1952 as campaign manager for John's victorious Senate race in Massachusetts, but he was uncertain about his own career path. He worked briefly at a number of jobs—in the Department of Justice's Criminal Division, on the Hoover Commission on Reorganization of the Executive Branch, and most importantly with the Senate Permanent Subcommittee on Investigations. By 1955, Kennedy had worked his way up to chief counsel to the Investigations Subcommittee, which examined waste, fraud, and mismanagement in the government. He quickly gained a reputation as a dedicated and uncompromising fighter against organized crime and corruption. The evidence he collected against powerful labor unions inspired the creation, in January 1957, of the

"I just didn't know anything when I got out of college. I wanted to do graduate work, but I didn't know whether to go to law school or business school. I had no attraction to business, so I entered law school."
—Robert F. Kennedy

Robert and John Kennedy worked together on the Senate Rackets Committee.

Select Committee on Improper Activities in the Labor or Management Field, otherwise known as the Rackets Committee. Kennedy served as chief counsel for the committee. One of his main targets was the famous Jimmy Hoffa, president of the Teamsters labor union. After resigning in 1959, Kennedy wrote a bestselling book called *The Enemy Within*, about his experiences in the Rackets Committee.

In 1960, Robert Kennedy became the manager of John's presidential campaign. In the closing days of the hard-fought race against Republican Richard Nixon, Martin Luther King Jr. was arrested in Atlanta, Georgia, for sitting at a white lunch counter. Several months before, King had been arrested for driving in Georgia with an Alabama license. With this second arrest, the Georgia judge denied him bail. Then, claiming King had violated

The large, powerful Teamsters union, which was composed mainly of truck drivers, had a history of crime and corruption in its leadership. Jimmy Hoffa (1913-1975), who ran the Teamsters from 1957 to 1971, was convicted of jury tampering and fraud and served four years in prison. He disappeared in 1975 and is believed to have been murdered.

bail: property or money given to obtain a release from legal custody

misdemeanor: a criminal offense less serious than a felony

his probation, he sentenced him to four months of hard labor. King was taken in chains to a state prison in rural Georgia, and his pregnant wife, Coretta Scott King, feared for his life. The Kings' friends and supporters contacted both presidential campaigns and demanded a response to the injustice. Nixon refused to comment publicly, but John Kennedy was aware that he desperately needed the black vote. Urged on by his advisers, he called Coretta King and offered his support.

Initially, Robert Kennedy believed that his brother's gesture would lose important white votes in the South. He became angry, however, that the judge had unfairly denied King bail on a misdemeanor charge. Robert called the judge and requested that King be freed from jail. King was released, and John F. Kennedy won the election with two-thirds of the black vote.

Robert Kennedy speaks to the press to promote his brother's presidential campaign.

On January 21, 1961, President Kennedy appointed his brother as attorney general of the United States. Robert was criticized for his youth (he was 35 years old), his lack of experience, and his close relationship with the president. He came to the cabinet, however, with more power and influence than any previous attorney general. He was John's most trusted adviser, and the president came to rely heavily on his brother's opinions—not only in law enforcement, but also in domestic and foreign affairs.

In the Cabinet

When Robert Kennedy began his tenure as attorney general, he did not place civil rights as a high priority; fighting organized crime and winning the Cold War seemed to be more important issues. Although Kennedy supported the goals of the civil rights movement, he did not always support its methods. He believed the best way for the Justice Department to create change was in the area of voting rights. Under Kennedy's leadership, the department brought 57 voting rights cases to court, many of them in Mississippi. In 1962, he was active in setting up the Voter Education Project, which distributed money from philanthropic foundations to various civil rights organizations to encourage voter registration. He also hired more black lawyers in the Justice Department. The civil rights movement was entering a new stage of activism, however, and Kennedy reluctantly found himself and his department involved in several dramatic and well-publicized events. As he dealt with one racial crisis after another, he gradually gained a better understanding of and sympathy with the struggles of America's blacks and other minorities.

In May 1961, a group of young black and white volunteers called Freedom Riders rode buses through the South to protest segregation in interstate travel. Segregation still existed in most Southern states, despite the fact that the Supreme Court had ruled it unconstitutional in 1960. The Freedom Riders risked their lives to draw attention to the

Before his arrest, Martin Luther King Jr. had not endorsed either presidential candidate, although Nixon had a much better record of supporting civil rights. The U.S. had never had a Catholic president, and as a Protestant minister, King distrusted Kennedy's Catholicism. After his release, King remained neutral, recognizing that Kennedy's action had been motivated mainly by politics. He remarked, however, "there are moments when the politically expedient is the morally wise." King's father, Martin Luther King Sr., had a stronger reaction: he wholeheartedly endorsed Kennedy, saying, "I'll take a Catholic or the Devil himself if he'll wipe the tears from my daughter-in-law's eyes. I've got a suitcase full of votes—my whole church—for . . . Senator Kennedy."

inequality in the South, hoping the Kennedy administration would step in. In Anniston and Birmingham, Alabama, Freedom Riders were dragged from their buses and beaten by white mobs; one of the buses was fire-bombed. Despite the danger, the Freedom Riders vowed to continue their journey through Alabama. Because the trip involved interstate travel and local officials had failed to act, protecting the lives of the Freedom Riders became an issue of federal responsibility. Robert Kennedy called the bus company to arrange for a new driver for the protesters, but the Alabama governor and other law-enforcement officers refused to control the violence. Another riot occurred when the bus arrived in Montgomery. John Siegenthaler, Kennedy's assistant in the Justice Department, was beaten unconscious with a metal pipe when he tried to rescue a woman from the mob.

Freedom Riders escape their burning bus in Anniston, Alabama.

The situation came to a head on May 21, as thousands of angry whites surrounded the First Baptist Church in Montgomery, where Martin Luther King was inside honoring the Freedom Riders. The crowd burned a car and threatened to set the church on fire. A bloodbath was avoided only after Kennedy sent in 500 federal marshals and, at Kennedy's insistence, the governor ordered in the National Guard. Once the situation in Montgomery was under control, Kennedy ordered the Interstate Commerce Commission to end segregation immediately in interstate bus terminals and then in railroad and airline terminals. By 1963, racial segregation was eliminated from interstate transportation facilities.

Meanwhile, another civil rights conflict was brewing. In January 1961, a black 29-year-old air force veteran named James Meredith had applied to the all-white University of Mississippi in Oxford. He was rejected and filed a lawsuit with the support of the NAACP. After numerous delays, the Supreme Court ruled in September 1962 that Meredith must be admitted. The governor of Mississippi, Ross Barnett, appeared on statewide television to declare that he would rather be jailed than allow a black person to attend the University of Mississippi. Meredith was turned away from the campus by officials on four separate occasions. The governor and lieutenant governor personally blocked Meredith's path, and they were cited for contempt by the United States Court of Appeals. Thousands of people gathered in Oxford to protest against Meredith.

The Meredith situation made Robert Kennedy realize how deeply ingrained segregation was in the South. On his brother's advice, President Kennedy federalized the Mississippi National Guard and ordered U.S. Army troops to stand by in Memphis, Tennessee. On September 30, federal marshals escorted Meredith to the edge of campus with the plan that he would register the next morning. That night, however, state officials unexpectedly withdrew the state police, leaving the marshals to protect Meredith from a crowd of several thousand hostile whites. During the night, the mob attacked the marshals, first throwing bricks and bottles, then resorting to gunshots and fire-bombs. A reporter and a local repairman were killed by stray bullets, and hundreds of people on both sides were injured. The rioting did not end until early morning, after U.S. Army troops began arriving in Oxford. James Meredith successfully registered at 8:00 A.M. on October 1, 1962. Robert Kennedy later said, "The idea that we got through the evening without the marshals being killed and without Meredith being killed was a miracle."

The incident in Mississippi confirmed the Kennedy administration's commitment to desegregation, but black leaders such as Martin Luther King Jr. believed it was only

"I am a graduate of the University of Mississippi," wrote James Meredith (b. 1933) to Robert Kennedy in September 1963. "For this I am proud of my country. . . . The question always arises—was it worth the cost? . . . I believe that I echo the feeling of most Americans when I say that 'no price is too high to pay for freedom of person, equality of opportunity, and human dignity.'"

a token victory. In the spring of 1963, King and his supporters decided to take their protests to the department stores and lunch counters of Birmingham, Alabama, one of the most segregated cities in the country. This effort marked a turning point in the civil rights movement. The graphic images of protesters being attacked by police dogs and pounded by water from high-pressure fire hoses were published and televised all over the country. On May 10, segregationists bombed King's brother's house and the motel where King and other civil rights leaders were staying. In response, angry blacks rioted in African American neighborhoods. By July 1963, racial demonstrations had occurred in nearly 200 American cities. In the wake of this violence, Robert Kennedy became convinced that strong civil rights legislation was necessary. He was ready to try to persuade the president of this need, even if it meant losing the support of Southern politicians.

In June 1963, Governor George Wallace of Alabama (who had declared, "Segregation now! Segregation tomorrow! Segregation forever!" in his January 1963 inaugural speech) attempted to stop the admission of two black students to the University of Alabama. Kennedy was ready to federalize the Alabama National Guard and send in regular army troops from Fort Benning, Georgia, if a confrontation occurred. Wallace personally blocked the students as they arrived to register. The Guard was federalized, but on the second try at registration on June 11, Wallace stepped aside. The students were registered and the University of Alabama was desegregated without any of the violence that had occurred in Oxford. That same night, however, NAACP leader Medgar Evers was murdered in the driveway of his home in Mississippi.

John F. Kennedy, at Robert's urging, appeared on television to address the nation on the evening of June 11. According to Assistant Attorney General Burke Marshall, every member of the cabinet was opposed to John making that speech. Robert, however, strongly believed that racial

Robert Kennedy testifies before the House Judiciary Committee during Congressional hearings on the Civil Rights bill. He urged his listeners to enact laws that would allow civil rights issues to be dealt with in court rather than through violent confrontations.

discrimination was a moral issue that needed to be confronted immediately, and the president agreed. After only a few hours of preparation, John Kennedy delivered a moving and strong message. "One hundred years of delay have passed since President Lincoln freed the slaves, yet their heirs, their grandsons, are not fully free," he declared. "Are we to say to the world—and much more importantly to each other—that this is the land of the free, except for the Negroes; that we have no second-class citizens, except Negroes?" A week later, the president sent Congress the strongest civil rights bill in history, giving the Justice Department massive power to go to court for black Americans to prevent discrimination and guarantee equal rights in all public facilities. The Civil Rights Act was passed one year later.

The Civil Rights Act of 1964

Robert Kennedy with Senate leaders Everett Dirksen of Illinois (center) and Hubert Humphrey of Minnesota watch from front-row seats at President Johnson signs historic civil rights legislation.

John F. Kennedy was assassinated just five months after submitting his civil rights legislation to Congress. When his successor, Lyndon B. Johnson, signed the act into law on July 2, 1964, it was as a tribute to President Kennedy.

As Robert Kennedy later described it, the Civil Rights Act of 1964 forbade the use "of literacy and other tests in such a way as to deny the right to vote to anyone on the basis of his race." It also banned racial discrimination in all public facilities and established free and equal use of all businesses open to the public—including hotels, restaurants, gas stations, theaters, and amusement parks. Furthermore, the act prohibited racial discrimination in employment and created an Equal Employment Opportunity Commission to investigate discrimination charges.

The attorney general and the Department of Justice were given the power to take legal action against public facilities and public schools that violated the act and failed to desegregate. During the remainder of the 1960s, actions were brought against more than 500 school districts and 400 public facilities. The constitutionality of the Civil Rights Act of 1964 was upheld by the Supreme Court in *Heart of Atlanta Motel v. United States* on December 14, 1964.

★ ★

Although the Civil Rights Act was a major step forward, African Americans still faced many obstacles to equality, and protests continued. In front of the Justice Department building in 1963, Robert Kennedy addressed a group of demonstrators who were protesting employment discrimination.

Despite their growing commitment to civil rights, the Kennedy brothers were not enthusiastic about Martin Luther King's proposed protest march on Washington, D.C., scheduled for August 1963. They thought such a demonstration would damage the chances for passage of the civil rights bill. But when they realized the march would go ahead anyway, Robert Kennedy helped ensure that it was as calm and orderly as possible. The Justice Department arranged for food, water, and portable toilets for the marchers, and it alerted police and nearby army troops in case violence occurred. On August 28, 250,000 people, both black and white, peacefully marched and gathered at the Lincoln Memorial to hear King's famous "I Have a Dream" speech.

Besides civil rights, the war against organized crime was the law-enforcement issue most important to Robert

Kennedy. During his tenure as attorney general, the Organized Crime and Racketeering Section of the Justice Department's Criminal Division quadrupled in size, and convictions against mobsters and racketeers rose substantially. Kennedy also helped to coordinate all Justice Department agencies (including the Bureau of Narcotics, the Internal Revenue Service, the Department of Labor, and the Immigration and Naturalization Service) in criminal investigations.

On November 22, 1963, President John F. Kennedy was shot and killed while riding in a motorcade in Dallas, Texas. His death shocked the nation, and Robert was overcome with grief. Although he stayed on as attorney general under President Lyndon Johnson, Robert's attachment to and identification with his brother had been so great that he found it difficult to work with John's successor. In June

On the day of John F. Kennedy's assassination, Robert Kennedy mourns with his brother's widow, Jacqueline, as the body is brought back to Washington from Dallas.

1964, he emerged from mourning, determined to continue John Kennedy's legacy. He set his sights on the open Senate seat in New York. Announcing his candidacy on August 22, Robert Kennedy resigned from his position as attorney general on September 2, 1964.

Looking Forward

Kennedy arose from the tragedy of his brother's assassination a changed man. Victorious in New York in 1964, he became "the senator for the young and the poor, the black and the brown, the sick and the old." Kennedy traveled the country, speaking out for the rights of the disadvantaged. He became a vocal supporter of Hispanic migrant workers, Native Americans, and inner-city and rural children. For

Robert Kennedy makes his acceptance speech after being nominated as a Senate candidate by the New York State Democrats. Behind him are his wife, Ethel, and their three-year-old daughter, Kerry.

instance, in 1966 Kennedy started the Bedford-Stuyvesant Restoration Project with the senior senator from New York, Jacob Javits. This section of Brooklyn was a large and very poor ghetto in which nearly half a million blacks and Puerto Ricans lived. Kennedy obtained support from private enterprise as well as charitable foundations and the federal government to create jobs and improve housing and health care.

As the Vietnam War escalated, Kennedy's opposition to it grew, and he openly disagreed with President Johnson's policies. He officially became a presidential candidate for the Democratic nomination on March 16, 1968. By the California primary on June 4 (which he won with 46 percent of the vote to Eugene McCarthy's 42 percent), Kennedy was emerging as the frontrunner for the Democratic presidential nomination, though the outcome was still very uncertain. After making his victory speech at the Ambassador Hotel in Los Angeles, he was leaving through the kitchen when he was shot in the head by Sirhan Sirhan, a 24-year-old Palestinian who believed Kennedy was an enemy of the Arab countries. Robert Kennedy died on June 6, 1968, at the age of 42. Americans mourned for the Kennedy family and were appalled by the terrible violence that had killed yet another political figure.

Some historians believe the assassination of Robert Kennedy changed the course of American history. If he had been elected president, America's involvement in Vietnam may have ended much sooner. His strong bond with blacks, the poor, and other minorities might have motivated him to do more to combat discrimination and poverty. Kennedy's legacy remained strong, however, as an activist attorney general who helped to shape new civil rights legislation and to desegregate schools and public facilities. He used his prominent position to vigorously promote justice and enforce the law for all Americans, regardless of color.

★ ★ 7 ★ ★

EDWIN MEESE III

Politicizing the Office

Ed Meese liked working in law enforcement. As a 33-year-old deputy district attorney in Alameda County, California, in 1964, he enjoyed trial work and even set his sights on being district attorney one day. Then an incident occurred that changed the course of his career and his life.

At the University of California at Berkeley, a large number of students promoted liberal causes such as nuclear disarmament, civil rights, and opposition to capital punishment. The university, however, did not allow political groups to operate on campus. Students began setting up tables, handing out pamphlets, signing up new members, and collecting petition signatures in a small area called the Bancroft strip, outside the main gate to the campus. Although the land technically belonged to the university, the students were allowed to use it. But as the political activity became more radical, state legislators and community groups pressured Berkeley administrators to ban students from organizing at the Bancroft strip. The university did so in September 1964, and the campus erupted in conflict. Student activists, some of whom had been in civil rights demonstrations in Mississippi, formed the Free Speech Movement to protest what they believed to be an act of censorship. Graduate students went on strike in support of the cause; even faculty members and more conservative students believed that the university was acting

Taking strong stances on controversial issues of the 1980s—including abortion, affirmative action, drugs, and school prayer—won Edwin Meese III (b. 1931) both praise and blame as the 75th attorney general.

115

unfairly. On December 2, between 4,000 and 5,000 people gathered to hear student leaders speak at a demonstration. Afterward, more than 1,000 held a sit-in occupying Sproul Hall, the main administration building on campus.

To many community members, this protest seemed an outrage perpetrated by a privileged group of college kids who attended a state university supported by taxpayers. On the advice of the district attorney of Alameda County, California governor Pat Brown ordered the police to Berkeley at 2 A.M. to clear the building. Deputy district attorney Ed Meese rushed to the scene as hundreds of California highway patrolmen and Alameda County sheriff's deputies converged onto the campus. During the next 12 hours, 773 people were arrested, many of whom nonviolently resisted efforts to remove them from the building.

Chanting "Freedom now," a Berkeley student is carried off to jail after participating in the sit-in at Sproul Hall.

It was the largest mass arrest in the history of California. Advising the police, Meese formulated a system in which each person was photographed and essential information was obtained. The students were then released on bail pending their trial. Meese also participated in prosecuting the students, calling the sit-in "a paramilitary operation." All were convicted of trespassing, but most received suspended sentences.

In 1966, Meese's strong position against campus demonstrations and student protesters brought him to the attention of the recently elected governor of California, Ronald Reagan, who had promised during his campaign to "clean up the mess in Berkeley." Reagan liked Meese's no-nonsense approach to maintaining order on campus and controlling riots and disturbances. The new governor offered him a job as extradition and clemency secretary in his administration. This was the beginning of a long relationship between Ronald Reagan and Ed Meese, which culminated in Meese becoming attorney general during Reagan's presidency in the 1980s. Meese was a controversial figure, intensely loyal to the president and sharing his conservative beliefs. During his tenure as attorney general, he actively worked to reshape the judicial branch of the federal government to reflect Reagan's political ideology. Along the way, he attracted praise, criticism, and even scandal. He became one of the best-known public officials of the Reagan administration—and the most investigated attorney general in U.S. history.

The mass arrests did not end the Free Speech Movement. After several more weeks of campus conflict, the administration lifted many of its restrictions on student political activity. After this victory, the Free Speech Movement eventually dissolved, but it was replaced by many other campus groups, especially antiwar ones, and student protests continued throughout the 1960s.

extradition: the surrender of someone charged with a crime for trial by one state or country to another

clemency: an act of mercy or forgiveness; willingness to lessen the severity of a punishment

conservative: one who generally believes in limiting, rather than expanding, the role of government in society

The Formative Years

Meese's great-grandfather, Hermann, came to the United States from Germany in 1850, traveled to San Francisco by wagon train, and finally settled in the city of Oakland in 1878. Edwin Meese, son of Hermann, was city councilman and treasurer of Oakland in the early 1900s. His son, Edwin Meese II, worked as a court clerk, then treasurer and tax collector for Alameda County. Edwin Meese III was born on December 2, 1931, the oldest of four sons of Edwin II and his wife, Leone. The Meeses were a middle-class Republican family who valued public service. Edwin III was a Boy Scout, and during World War II, he and his brothers published a neighborhood newspaper and used the profits to buy war bonds.

Edwin Meese III was an intelligent young man who was valedictorian of his high school class and earned a college scholarship to Yale University in Connecticut. He solidified his conservative views as a member of the Yale Political Union. After obtaining his B.A. degree in 1953, Meese returned to northern California to attend law school at Berkeley. During his legal studies, he took time off to serve in the army for two years as a lieutenant in military intelligence. He returned to Berkeley and earned his law degree in 1958, then married his high school sweetheart, Ursula Herrick. They would eventually have three children together.

Meese was always fascinated with law enforcement and police work. Considering the family tradition of public service, it was natural that he headed to the district attorney's office after getting his law degree. During his eight years as deputy district attorney in Alameda County, Meese helped to develop a drug abuse testing program and was a liaison to the grand jury. In his spare time, he rode in patrol cars with police officers. The United States Junior Chamber of Commerce named Meese one of the outstanding young men in America in 1965. In addition to his much-publicized involvement in prosecuting the Berkeley Free Speech Movement, Meese also helped to control and disperse anti-draft protests at Berkeley and in Oakland.

Once Meese joined Ronald Reagan's staff in early 1967, he advised the governor on issues of law enforcement, capital punishment, and campus disturbances. He was quickly promoted from extradition and clemency secretary to legal affairs secretary, and then—from 1969 to 1974—served as Reagan's executive assistant and chief of staff. At the request of the governor, Meese developed a system for assessing judicial candidates by establishing three-member evaluation panels in each county. He also prepared all Reagan's speeches to law-enforcement groups. The two men shared the same conservative views on major issues, and they became very close personal friends.

Meese believed that campus unrest threatened academic freedom and prevented law-abiding students from continuing their studies. He felt that antiwar protesters hindered America's effort in Vietnam and ended up prolonging the war. Meese was on the scene at antiwar protests in 1967 at the Army Induction Center in Oakland, as well as when violence broke out in 1969 at the San Francisco State and Berkeley campuses. At San Francisco State, Meese took charge and arrested the leaders of the campus demonstrations. At Berkeley, Meese advised Reagan to send in National Guard troops to control rioting protesters who were demanding a piece of land to be used as a people's park. One person had been killed and many injured in conflicts with police and highway patrol officers. The governor declared a state of emergency and ordered in the National Guard, which sent a helicopter to blanket the campus with tear gas. The Guard stayed in Berkeley for 17 days, until order was restored.

When Reagan left office in 1974, Meese worked in the private sector. In 1975 and 1976, he served as vice president for administration at Rohr Industries, an aerospace company near San Diego. After a short time in private law practice, Meese began teaching courses on criminal law at the University of San Diego, where he was also director of the Center for Criminal Justice Policy and Management.

In 1979, Meese joined Ronald Reagan's campaign for the 1980 Republican presidential nomination. With Meese as chief of staff, Reagan won the Republican nomination and then swept to victory in the election, defeating the Democratic incumbent, Jimmy Carter. Reagan appointed Meese to a new cabinet position, counselor to the president.

On January 21, 1981, his first day as president, Reagan meets with (left to right) Deputy Chief of Staff Michael Deaver, Meese, Chief of Staff James Baker, and Press Secretary James Brady in the Oval Office.

independent counsel:
a nonpartisan attorney approved by representatives of both major parties to conduct a thorough investigation of a particular event or individual

Meese served as the president's chief policy adviser and was a member of the National Security Council. He was also responsible for administration of the cabinet and the daily operations of the executive branch.

After Reagan was elected to his second term, he appointed Meese as his attorney general. The confirmation hearings in the Senate took 13 months to complete while an independent counsel investigated irregularities in Meese's financial affairs. Meese was not indicted on any of the charges, however, and he was confirmed as attorney general on February 23, 1985.

In the Cabinet

Ronald Reagan had come to office with such a well-defined policy program and worked so actively to implement it that his tenure was often called "the Reagan Revolution." As attorney general, Meese believed his main function was to further Reagan's agenda in the Justice Department. He pursued legal issues supported by the administration and challenged policies opposed by the administration. For his actions, he was often accused of "unabashed partisanship" and politicizing the office of attorney general. Meese, however, was determined to act according to his principles and support his president in all matters. "This department will be fiercely independent in . . . upholding the law," he said at his March 1985 swearing-in ceremony. "But this is not inconsistent with conscientiously and vigorously implementing the president's philosophy, which is the mainstream of today's American political thinking."

Ronald Reagan consulted with Meese on many matters during the years they worked together.

★
John Mitchell: Partisanship and Prison

John Mitchell, who served during the Richard Nixon administration from 1969 to 1972, had several things in common with Edwin Meese. Both were close friends and advisers of the presidents they served, both were political conservatives who had similar approaches to their jobs, and both became embroiled in controversy and scandal.

Like Meese, Mitchell viewed the office of attorney general as a means of supporting presidential policy. Under his direction, the Justice Department challenged court-ordered busing, filing an amicus brief that opposed the Supreme Court's decision to integrate a school district. In *Alexander v. Holmes* (1969) and similar cases, the Justice Department refused to implement the Court's decision ordering immediate desegregation. In protest of this policy, one-quarter of the attorneys in the Civil Rights Division resigned.

Mitchell attacked the Supreme Court in a series of speeches calling for judicial restraint. He declared that judges who "substitute their will for the people's will" had no place in a democracy. With Mitchell's help in the selection process, Nixon successfully appointed conservative Warren Burger to the Supreme Court. The nominations of conservatives Clement Haynesworth and Harold Carswell, however, met with

John Mitchell (1913-1988) meets with President Richard Nixon (left) in the White House.

such strong opposition in the Senate, as well as from organized labor and civil rights groups, that moderate Harry Blackmun was appointed instead.

Mitchell resigned as attorney general in 1972 to head up President Nixon's reelection campaign. Then a series of scandals occurred that linked Nixon and his administration to the burglary of Democratic Party headquarters at the Watergate apartment and office complex in Washington, D.C. This break-in and the subsequent cover-up were tied to Nixon's reelection committee, members of the president's staff, and eventually Nixon himself, who resigned from office on August 9, 1974.

Mitchell denied involvement in the Watergate scandal, but evidence indicated that he approved the break-in and also helped pay off defendants to keep them quiet. On January 15, 1975, Mitchell was found guilty of conspiracy, obstruction of justice, and perjury. He became the first attorney general to do time in prison, serving 19 months in Montgomery, Alabama, before being released on January 19, 1979. Disbarred from practicing law, John Mitchell died in Washington, D.C., in November 1988.

Nixon's successor, Gerald Ford, appointed legal scholar Edward Levi as attorney general in an attempt to reestablish the integrity and nonpartisanship of the office. But the Watergate scandal had convinced the public of the need for someone outside the executive branch to investigate accusations against powerful government officials. In 1978, President Jimmy Carter signed the Ethics in Government Act, a package of reforms that included a law providing for the appointment of a special prosecutor to fill this role. The attorney general was to recommend the appointment of a special prosecutor to examine misconduct charges against officials in certain executive branch positions. The special prosecutor would be appointed by a panel of three judges at the U.S. Court of Appeals in Washington, D.C.

This law was invoked 11 times between 1978 and 1982, resulting in the appointments of three special prosecutors. In 1983, the law was revised to reduce the number of officials it covered. It also gave the attorney general more power over whether to request a special prosecutor and over removing an unsatisfactory prosecutor. Finally, the term "special prosecutor" was changed to a more neutral one, "independent counsel."

Although he opposed the independent counsel law, believing it was unconstitutional and undermined the ability of the Department of Justice, President Ronald Reagan signed it on January 3, 1983. Independent counsels would be appointed to investigate Reagan administration officials on seven separate occasions. Ironically, the first person to be investigated under the new law was Reagan's attorney general nominee, Edwin Meese.

★ ★

Meese publicly challenged many of the decisions of the U.S. Supreme Court, emphasizing "the need to protect and preserve basic constitutional values." He thought that the Court should interpret the law according to the "original intent" of the Constitution and not become a social or political policymaker. "Where the language of the Constitution is specific, it must be obeyed," he explained. "Where there is ambiguity as to the precise meaning . . . it should be interpreted and applied in a manner so as to at least not contradict the text of the Constitution itself." Some Supreme Court justices did not agree with this doctrine of judicial restraint, however. Liberal justice William Brennan believed it was "little more than arrogance" to think that someone could "gauge accurately the intent of the framers" of the Constitution. He argued that "current Justices read the Constitution in the only way that we can: as twentieth century Americans," and added, "The ultimate question must be, what do the words of the text mean in our time?"

Specifically, Meese attacked the Supreme Court's 1966 ruling in *Miranda v. Arizona*, which required the police to advise criminal suspects of their legal rights before questioning, and the 1961 *Mapp v. Ohio* decision, which blocked the use of illegally seized evidence in a trial. Meese felt that both these rulings expanded the rights of the suspects and aided the guilty. Meese also denounced the 1973 *Roe v. Wade* opinion, which struck down most legal restrictions on abortion. The Department of Justice, under Meese's direction, filed briefs that proposed reversing the momentous decision. "The textual, doctrinal and historical basis for *Roe v. Wade* is so far flawed," declared one brief, "and . . . is a source of such instability in the law that this court should reconsider that decision." The Department of Justice filed amicus briefs in *Wallace v. Jaffree* (1985) to allow silent prayer in public schools, and in *Bethel School District v. Fraser* (1986) to allow searches and other restrictions of First Amendment rights of students. Under Meese, the

"**N**either *Mapp* nor *Miranda* helps any innocent person. They only help guilty people."
—Edwin Meese

Justice Department also opposed affirmative action and supported cases that disputed minority hiring quotas. The majority of Meese's challenges, however, were rejected by the courts.

In addition, Meese questioned the authority of the Supreme Court and whether its decisions were the law of the land and binding on all state and federal officials. He stated that a Supreme Court decision "binds the parties in a case and also the executive branch for whatever enforcement is necessary. But such a decision does not establish a 'supreme law of the land' that is binding on all persons and parts of government, henceforth and forevermore." Such remarks touched off a debate about judicial power. Conservatives asserted that the Founding Fathers never intended the Supreme Court to have such power. In response, Ira Glasser, the executive director of the American Civil Liberties Union (ACLU), called Meese "the most radical and dangerous attorney general in this century." Others worried that if people opposed Court rulings, there would be excessive litigation, the rule of law would be undermined, and the system would be disrupted.

Another important priority for Meese and the Reagan administration was reshaping the judiciary through the selection of conservative judges. During the eight years of his presidency, Reagan appointed judges for nearly half of all federal judiciary positions, including 292 federal district court judges, 83 appellate court judges, and 3 Supreme Court justices—Sandra Day O'Connor, Antonin Scalia, and Anthony Kennedy. Meese was closely involved in the selection process, and he made it much more thorough than previous administrations had done. Candidates faced a 10-page questionnaire, a daylong interview at the Justice Department, examination by a special committee, and then approval by the attorney general before the president made the final decision. This method ensured that the chosen judges had a high level of competence, but the main goal was "ideological screening"—finding judges who were not

affirmative action: governmental efforts to improve the job or educational opportunities of minority groups and women

The American Civil Liberties Union (ACLU) is a non-partisan organization whose aim is to preserve, extend, and defend basic rights and civil liberties as stated in the Constitution. The organization focuses on freedoms of speech, press, and assembly; due process; and equality under the law for all people.

Sandra Day O'Connor (b. 1930), the first female justice of the Supreme Court, was sworn in by Chief Justice Warren Burger (left) on September 25, 1981, as her husband, John, looked on.

only legally qualified, but who also had a judicial philosophy that mirrored the president's (and Meese's own) beliefs in judicial restraint and original intent. When accused of politicizing the courts, Meese replied that the president simply wanted "to ensure that they [judges] played a truly judicial role, rather than usurping the authority of the elected branches of our constitutional system." These judges, Meese said, would "return this country's judicial system to the path intended by the founding fathers."

Meese tackled a number of other issues during his term as attorney general. Believing that an essential function of the government was to protect Americans from crime, he cracked down on violence, drugs, and pornography. Meese argued for more prisons and tougher prison sentences. He visited more than 20 countries to promote international cooperation against drug trafficking and terrorism, and during this period both the rate of drug use and the number of terrorist incidents in the United States dropped. In 1985 alone, the FBI detected and prevented 23 different terrorist missions in the U.S. Meese also established an Obscenity Enforcement Unit in the Justice Department to investigate and prosecute child pornography offenses.

By 1988, however, Ed Meese was facing two more investigations for questionable conduct. The Reagan administration had been shaken by the Iran-Contra affair, in which it was discovered that the U.S. government illegally used the proceeds from sales of weapons to Iran to fund anticommunist rebels (called "contras") in Nicaragua. The Justice Department's initial investigation of the scandal was weak, and Meese was accused of being involved in

Stacks of cocaine seized by federal agents as part of a nationwide effort to end cultivation and sales of the drug.

President Reagan motions to Attorney General Meese during a November 11, 1986, White House press briefing on the Iran-Contra affair.

the scheme and subsequent cover-up. He then faced separate charges that he had helped a personal friend obtain lucrative government contracts and had violated standards of ethical conduct. An independent counsel, James McKay, conducted a 14-month investigation into Meese's numerous transactions. Although McKay found that Meese had violated telecommunications laws and the code of the Internal Revenue Service, the counsel concluded that there was insufficient evidence and announced he would not recommend criminal prosecution for misconduct. By this time, public opinion had turned against the attorney general; one poll found that 55 percent of Americans (including half of those who described themselves as conservative) believed Meese should resign. Meese claimed that McKay's report vindicated him, but he announced his resignation as attorney general on July 5, 1988, and left office in early August.

Looking Forward

After leaving the Reagan administration, Edwin Meese pursued a career as a lecturer, writer, and consultant specializing in criminal and constitutional law, the Reagan presidency, national security, law enforcement, and criminal justice. He became a Distinguished Visiting Fellow at the Hoover Institution at Stanford University, a Ronald Reagan Distinguished Fellow in Public Policy at the Heritage Foundation in Washington, and a Distinguished Senior Fellow at the Institute of United States Studies at the University of London. His most recent articles have dealt with terrorism and national security.

Meese's tenure as attorney general was tainted with controversy and scandal. But regardless of how history may judge his participation in the Reagan cabinet, there is no doubt that he had a profound effect on the Justice Department of the 1980s. With his strong convictions and public activism, he highlighted the increasingly political nature of the office of attorney general. To liberals and conservatives alike, Meese's enduring legacy may be the hundreds of conservative judges he helped to appoint, whose decisions continue to impact the significant issues of the twenty-first century.

★ ★ *8* ★ ★

JANET RENO

First Female Attorney General

It was 1960 when 22-year-old Janet Reno arrived in Cambridge, Massachusetts, to study law at Harvard University. Founded in 1817, the law school was intimidating, prestigious, and intensely competitive. Reno was one of only 16 women in a class of 525 students. Women had been admitted to study law at Harvard since 1950, but little had been done to make them feel welcome. A number of professors were hostile and suspicious toward female students. One said he wouldn't call on them in big classrooms because their voices were too soft to be heard. There was only one women's restroom in the entire law school, and it was located in the basement of a building where few classes were held. Many of the male students believed that Reno and other women just took up spaces that should have been filled by men. Even the dean admitted that "he did not know what we were going to do with our legal educations," recalled Reno.

By 1993, Harvard had made significant progress in equality for women. About 40 percent of the law students were female, and there were equal numbers of men's and women's bathrooms in most of the buildings. That same year, Janet Reno was sworn in as the first female attorney general of the United States. Shortly after assuming office, Reno discovered that her old Harvard tax professor, Ernest Brown, was now her employee; he worked in the Justice

Janet Reno (b. 1938), the 78th attorney general, was at the center of major news events throughout the 1990s.

131

Department's Tax Division as a senior consultant. When she went to his office to greet him, Brown said he was "delighted" to have Reno as his boss.

The Formative Years

Janet Reno was born on July 21, 1938, in Miami, Florida, the oldest of four children of Henry and Jane Reno. Henry was an immigrant from Denmark whose father had changed his name in 1913 from Rasmussen to Reno, after the city in Nevada. Henry was a police reporter for the Miami *Herald*, and Jane worked as an investigative reporter for the Miami *News* after the children started school. Janet was most influenced by her strong, independent, and outspoken mother. In 1948, Jane built the three-bedroom family house, located at the edge of the Everglades south of Miami, entirely by herself. It would be Janet Reno's home until her appointment as attorney general 35 years later. "That house is a symbol to me," she declared, "that you can do anything you really want if it's the right thing to do and you put your mind to it."

In 1952, Janet entered Coral Gables High School in Miami-Dade County, where she was an excellent student, a champion debater, and a top athlete in softball and basketball. After graduating in 1956, she attended Cornell University in Ithaca, New York. She received a partial scholarship and worked part-time jobs as a waitress and dorm monitor to make ends meet. During summer breaks, Janet's father arranged for her to work as a clerk in the Miami-Dade County sheriff's department. She wanted to major in prelaw, but she focused on chemistry to please her mother, who wanted Janet to be a doctor. Soon, however, Janet was elected president of the Women's Student Government Association, and her interest in politics increased. After she graduated with a bachelor's degree in chemistry in 1960, she entered Harvard Law School with her mother's blessing.

Janet Reno's years at Harvard provided her with what she called "the best educational experience I ever had.

"**M**y mother always told me to do my best, to think my best, and to do right and consider myself a person."
—Janet Reno

Janet Reno's father died in 1967. Janet and her mother, Jane, continued to live together in the family home until Jane's death in December 1992—just two months before Janet's nomination as attorney general.

"**T**he courtrooms of the Dade County Courthouse . . . were like magical places to me when I went with my father as he covered trials, both criminal and civil. And I thought that one of the most wonderful things that anybody could do was to be a lawyer."
—Janet Reno

Those classes . . . really taught me how to think. And I believe that the way I approach problems . . . is due to the training I got from some extraordinary professors." Reno received her law degree from Harvard in 1963 and obtained a position as an associate for the Miami firm of Brigham and Brigham, which specialized in property law. Over the next four years, Reno handled real-estate cases and frequently appeared in court.

An ardent admirer of Senator—and former attorney general—Robert F. Kennedy, Reno joined the Miami Young Democrats. It was there that she met Gerald Lewis, becoming involved as a volunteer in his campaign for the state legislature in 1966. Lewis won the election, and shortly thereafter, he and Reno formed their own law firm, which handled wills, real estate, taxes, and business matters.

In 1971, Reno left the firm to begin a career in public service. She was hired as general counsel to the Florida House Judiciary Committee, helped revise the state's court system, and was the author of Florida's no-fault divorce law. The following year, she ran for the state legislature from Miami-Dade County. Though Reno beat five other Democrats in the primary, she lost to the Republican candidate by a narrow margin in the general election. After that, Reno worked as an assistant to the state attorney in Miami-Dade from 1973 to 1976, setting up a Juvenile Division to deal specifically with younger offenders. She also worked as a consultant to the senate committee revising the Florida criminal code.

Reno left the state attorney's office in 1976 and went back to private practice as a partner with Steel, Hector & Davis, a firm that had rejected her 14 years earlier because she was a woman. She tried civil suits and served pro bono on the board of directors of the Greater Miami Legal Services Corporation, which gave legal aid to the poor. When the Miami-Dade state attorney retired in January 1978, the Florida governor appointed 39-year-old Janet Reno as his replacement until the November election. She

pro bono: legal work done by lawyers free of charge

thus became the first female state attorney in Florida's history, presiding over an office with a budget of almost $4.5 million. As Miami-Dade's top prosecutor, Reno headed an office of 286 employees, 91 of them attorneys, who handled 40,000 misdemeanors and 15,000 felonies a year.

When Reno ran as a Democratic candidate to continue as state attorney, she received 76 percent of the vote in the Democratic primary. There was no Republican contender, so she won the election. She served in her position for the next 15 years, reelected for four straight terms as a Democrat in a heavily Republican area. She hired more women and developed and supported programs that were aimed at preventing and prosecuting child abuse, drug abuse, and domestic violence. While cracking down on drug smugglers and violent crime, Reno created a Drug Court that gave second chances to first-time offenders. She prosecuted cases of spouse and child abuse even if the victim did not press charges, and she set up shelters for battered women. She assigned lawyers to collect overdue child-support payments from "deadbeat dads," and collections of overdue payments doubled during the first year of the program. To help crime victims understand the legal process, Reno created a victim advocacy program staffed with trained counselors. She also helped to improve conditions in low-income housing by filing lawsuits against landlords who violated building codes. In addition, she supported a wide variety of health care and education programs as a means of preventing crime.

Despite all this activity, Reno was criticized for a below-average rate of convictions. In particular, she was blamed for failing to obtain a conviction against five white police officers charged with the beating death of a handcuffed, unarmed black man named Arthur McDuffie. After the policemen were all acquitted in May 1980, riots broke out in black communities throughout Miami. During four days of rioting, 16 people died and hundreds were injured. More than 1,000 people were arrested, and damages were

estimated at more than $200 million. After being con-
demned for being anti-police because she prosecuted the
officers in the first place, Reno was blamed by black groups
for losing the trials. Over the years, however, Reno's successes in dealing with Miami's crime problem won over
her critics. She became known as a tough, no-nonsense
prosecutor who also cared about social issues. Her focus on
juvenile justice and her support of family and community
concerns helped win her respect and popularity among all
ethnic groups.

After President Bill Clinton was elected in 1992, he had
trouble filling the last remaining cabinet position of his
new administration—the office of attorney general. His
first nominee, a corporate lawyer named Zoë Baird, was

Reno's office won criminal convictions resulting in 103 death sentences—despite her personal opposition to capital punishment.

A Democrat elected president in 1992 with strong support from women voters, Bill Clinton was determined to appoint the first female attorney general.

dropped after she admitted to hiring an illegal immigrant as a live-in nanny. Clinton's second nominee, Kimba Wood, a federal judge from New York, had hired an undocumented worker as a babysitter. Senator Joseph Biden, chair of the Senate Judiciary Committee, advised Clinton to look for an experienced prosecutor with a spotless reputation. On February 11, 1993, President Clinton nominated Janet Reno as the 78th attorney general of the United States. The Senate confirmed her quickly, and Reno was sworn in on March 12 in the Roosevelt Room at the White House. That afternoon, she was in her new office at the Justice Department, ready to go to work.

In the Cabinet

The new attorney general was immediately involved in a potentially disastrous situation inherited from her predecessor. The resolution of this crisis, on her 38th day on the job, would bring Reno harsh criticism and instant recognition throughout the country.

In February, local police in Waco, Texas, had alerted the Bureau of Alcohol, Tobacco, and Firearms (ATF) that a cult calling itself the Branch Davidians, headed by a zealot named David Koresh, was stockpiling weapons in a compound of buildings outside Waco. The police had received reports of federal gun law violations and the accumulation of an arsenal of assault weapons, ammunition, and explosives. The ATF attempted to search the premises with a warrant on February 28. This action resulted in a deadly gun battle in which four ATF agents and six cult members were killed.

President Clinton ordered the FBI to take over, and agents were set up around the outside of the compound. The FBI's Hostage Rescue Team of special negotiators was sent to Waco in an attempt to convince Koresh to give up, or to at least let the women and children out of the compound. Koresh refused, and a standoff followed. Koresh repeatedly promised the FBI he would surrender, but he continued to break his word and the days soon passed into weeks. "The FBI kept negotiating, kept trying every way they knew how to talk Koresh into leaving, but he never gave them a specific date," stated Reno, who closely monitored the situation from Washington after taking office on the 12th day of the standoff. The FBI had almost 950 talks with Koresh or his aides, a total of 215 hours of conversation. Local sheriffs and lawyers attempted to persuade him to leave. They managed to get him to release 37 people, including 21 children.

By the seventh week, the Hostage Rescue Team, which had been on constant alert, was near exhaustion. Reno was concerned for the safety of the remaining children inside the compound after allegations of sexual and physical abuse were reported. She also worried about the increasingly irrational behavior of David Koresh, who had sent the FBI letters in which he declared, "I am your God and you will bow under my feet." Cult members who had escaped the compound reported the accumulation of garbage and human waste, as well as the decaying corpses of those killed on February 28 inside the building. They also confirmed that Koresh and his followers had huge amounts of food and water that would allow them to hold out for months.

In mid-April, Reno was presented with a plan by the FBI to end the siege by using tear gas that stung the eyes, nose, and throat. The FBI planned to gradually pump the gas inside one end of the compound to get the cult members to leave. Reno discussed the use of tear gas with experts and was assured it would not cause any permanent harm to the children inside. She also spoke to U.S. Army officials, who recommended releasing tear gas over the entire compound at once. Reno stuck by the original plan, hoping to keep casualties to a minimum and reduce any panic. She gave the go-ahead for April 19, 1993, but ordered FBI agents not to fire at the compound even if fired upon, and to back off if a child was threatened at any

FBI agents used a wide variety of strategies to try to end the standoff. They sent in cartons of milk for the children, along with blank videotapes that Koresh was supposed to use to film the children and prove they were healthy. He did not comply, but the objects contained tiny bugging devices that allowed agents to hear conversations inside the compound. The FBI also waged psychological warfare on the cult members, trying to wear down or distract them by playing loud music, flashing bright lights, and cutting off electricity.

The Branch Davidians had lived outside of Waco for almost 60 years before the burning of their compound in 1993. Koresh, their leader since 1988, foretold a violent confrontation with the government—a final battle that would end the world and grant his followers eternal glory.

time. She notified President Clinton of her decision, and he expressed his approval and support. Agents announced to Koresh in advance that they would be using tear gas, again asking him to leave with the others. The Branch Davidians responded with gunfire.

At about 6 A.M., two armored vehicles with long steel noses approached the buildings, punched a hole through a wall, and began pumping in tear gas. "Come out now and you will not be harmed," shouted the agents. Inside the compound, the cult members put on gas masks and continued to fire their weapons. Soon, more armored vehicles began to pump gas into other parts of the compound. Still no one came out. Around noon, people inside spread kerosene and lamp oil. Then they ignited fires that resulted in several large explosions of the ammunition stores they had collected inside. Flames were visible from the outside, but no one came out. A few people were finally spotted and agents ran to save them. Winds as high as 30 miles per hour spread the flames throughout the compound. Approximately 75 cult members, including Koresh, and 25 children died in the flames. Just nine people—all adults—survived, and four of them were badly burned.

The FBI action had been a failure, and Janet Reno assumed complete responsibility. At 5:00 P.M. she held a press conference and announced to the nation, "I approved the plan, and I'm responsible for it. . . . I have absolutely no doubt at all that the cult members set [the fires] based on all the information that has been furnished to me. . . . I made the decisions. . . . The buck stops with me." Reno repeated this statement on every television network that night. There were calls for Reno to resign, but Clinton supported her and her popularity with the public soared. Despite the disastrous results of her decision, people were impressed by the way Reno handled herself. A *Time* magazine headline proclaimed, "The Capital is All Agog at the New Attorney General's Outspoken Honesty." By July, Reno's approval rating was 54 percent, higher than the president's.

FBI investigators discovered that 14 adults and 6 children had killed themselves or been murdered by gunshots, stabbing, or head trauma before the fire. They concluded that the cult members deliberately started the fire in three different areas of the compound. Clouds of suspicion still surrounded the Justice Department's actions, however. Six years later, in 1999, FBI and Justice Department officials admitted that some flammable tear gas canisters had been used at Waco. Reno had been assured that such devices had not been used, and she angrily called for an immediate inquiry. An independent 10-month investigation concluded in July 2000 that several hours before the fire, "potentially incendiary tear gas rounds were fired," and that some government officials had failed to disclose that fact at the time. It was also determined, however, that the tear gas rounds landed "harmlessly 75 feet from the living quarters," that federal agents did not fire any gunshots, and that they did not start the fire that destroyed the compound. Federal officials were also cleared of charges in a civil lawsuit brought by Branch Davidian survivors and their families. Finally, seven years after the siege, Janet Reno, the FBI, and the Justice Department were completely cleared of any wrongdoing in the Waco standoff.

Controversy continued to follow Reno during her time in the cabinet. Neither a close friend nor a former associate of the president (as many other attorney generals had been throughout history), Reno maintained her independence from Bill Clinton. She never hesitated to initiate investigations of other cabinet members, the first lady, and even the president himself when she suspected possible wrongdoing. Despite their distant relationship, Clinton asked Reno to stay on as attorney general during his second term after he was reelected in 1996. Criticized by fellow Democrats as not being loyal to the administration, Reno was also accused by Republicans of being too partisan when she refused to name an independent counsel to investigate Democratic fundraising practices in the 1996 elections. No matter what her course of action, Reno was attacked by one party or the other, but she always stood firm in her decisions.

Reno made international headlines in late 1999 with the Elian Gonzalez case. The six-year-old Cuban boy was found clinging to an inner tube in the waters off Fort Lauderdale, Florida, on Thanksgiving Day. Elian's mother and 10 other Cubans had drowned when their 16-foot motorboat capsized as they attempted to reach the United States. American authorities turned Elian over to his great-

Although Janet Reno had a cordial relationship with President Clinton, she remained an outsider in the world of Washington politics, becoming one of the most independent attorneys general in the history of the office.

Reno dealt with the legal issues surrounding immigration throughout her tenure, even before the Elian Gonzalez case brought them to the forefront. Here, she, Clinton, and other officials listen as a member of the U.S. Border Patrol (standing) gives a briefing on immigration in 1995.

uncle, Lazaro Gonzalez, and other relatives in Miami while the Justice Department's Immigration and Naturalization Service (INS) determined his fate.

The boy's father, Juan Miguel Gonzalez, who lived in Cuba, demanded that the United States return his son. Elian's American relatives argued that it had been the wish of the boy's mother for him to live in America and requested custody. Elian became an international celebrity, and the emotional impact of the case threatened to obscure the rule of law. Cuban Americans strongly believed Elian should grow up in freedom and not be returned to communist Cuba. A number of U.S. government officials, including the governor of Florida, Jeb Bush, and the vice president of the United States, Al Gore, also thought Elian should stay. The law was clear, however, and the INS ruled accordingly: only the boy's father could speak for him, and Juan Gonzales had the right to be reunited with his child. Janet Reno upheld the decision.

There were angry protests and demonstrations in Miami, directed against the attorney general and the Clinton administration. Reno repeatedly tried to talk Elian's Miami relatives into voluntarily turning the boy over to authorities, but they refused to cooperate and took the case to court. Both the federal district court and the state family court ruled in favor of the INS, but the relatives still delayed giving up Elian. Finally, on the morning

The boy at the center of an international custody battle, young Elian Gonzalez plays in the Florida sunshine.

of April 22, 2000, Reno ordered federal agents to forcibly take Elian Gonzalez from his relatives. Armed INS officers entered the home before dawn and within three minutes carried Elian out to a waiting government van. Hours later, the boy was reunited with his father at Andrews Air Force Base near Washington, D.C., and eventually they returned to Cuba. Although the Miami Cuban community opposed the action taken by Reno and a number of politicians called for an investigation of the incident, much of the American public supported the attorney general.

When Reno left office in January 2001, she was the second-longest-serving attorney general in history (only William Wirt served longer). "Janet Reno is the embodiment of integrity," declared Deputy Attorney General Eric Holder Jr. "She has consistently demonstrated the ability to make tough, and sometimes unpopular, decisions." During her eight years in office, Reno was subjected to intense criticism from both ends of the political spectrum. Crime dropped sharply while she was in office, however, and the American public held her in the highest esteem of all Clinton administration officials.

Looking Forward

After leaving office, Janet Reno returned to her family home in South Florida. Although she had been diagnosed with Parkinson's disease, a brain disorder, in 1995, she suffered few symptoms and remained politically active. She ran for governor of Florida in 2002, losing in the Democratic primary. Afterward, Reno continued to focus her attention on improving the public school system, protecting children, supporting senior citizen issues such as prescription drug benefits, safeguarding the environment, and promoting election reform. In April 2003, she told an interviewer that she spent her time "speaking, writing, trying to put my thoughts in order in terms of some of the issues that I want to address and also trying to improve my kayaking."

Before Reno became attorney general, her top priority had been reform and prevention programs dealing with juvenile and drug offenders. While she was in office, however, these issues were overshadowed by critical events that required her to make one controversial decision after another. Her tough choices made her one of the most recognized and scrutinized public figures of her time. Yet there was only one regret she voiced when asked if she would have done anything differently: "I would not have done what I did at Waco," she declared. The choice she had faced—between protecting individual freedoms and trying to save human lives—was one that had haunted attorneys general throughout history, and the issue would only intensify in the twenty-first century.

Vying to become the Democratic candidate for Florida governor, Janet Reno greeted her supporters before a debate in August 2002.

Attacks on America

During Janet Reno's tenure as attorney general, two shocking attacks occurred on U.S. soil that alerted Americans to the horror of terrorism. The World Trade Center bombing on February 26, 1993, masterminded by Muslim extremists, killed 6 people and injured more than 1,000. The Oklahoma City bombing on April 19, 1995, planned and carried out by American citizens, killed 168 people. In both instances, the FBI and the Justice Department, under Reno's direction, apprehended those responsible.

It was approximately 12:18 P.M. when a bomb exploded in a cargo van parked in the ramp beneath the World Trade Center in New York City. The bomb created a crater about 150 feet wide and five floors deep in the parking basement. A fragment of the van that was recovered revealed an identification number. It was soon determined that the van was a Ryder rental from Jersey City. The customer who rented it, Mohammad Salameh, had reported it stolen. Salameh then repeatedly called the rental office to try to get back his $400 deposit. When Salameh appeared at the office in person, FBI agents arrested him.

A subsequent search of Salameh's home and property led officials to the discovery of a bomb factory in Jersey City and resulted in the eventual arrest and conviction of several other bombers. Salameh and three coconspirators were sentenced to 240 years of imprisonment with no possibility of parole. In addition, Sheik Omar Abdel Rahman and nine others who were part of a global radical Muslim terrorist group were convicted of joining in the plot and also conspiring to destroy other New York landmarks.

Two years after the World Trade Center bombing, a massive truck bomb exploded in front of the Alfred P. Murrah Federal Building in Oklahoma City. Officials determined that the bomb was a mixture of fertilizer and fuel oil placed in the back of a rental truck. The blast blew off the front of the nine-story building, burying people under slabs of concrete and steel. Rescue workers pulled bodies from the rubble for two weeks; many of the dead were children from the building's daycare center.

Most people initially assumed that this bombing was also the work of Muslim extremists. As in the World Trade Center case, investigators found a piece of the bombers' truck inscribed with a serial number and traced it to a Ryder rental office. The man who rented the truck, however, turned out to be an American citizen—a 27-year-old U.S. Army veteran named Timothy McVeigh. Coincidentally, McVeigh had been pulled over by an Oklahoma state trooper just 90 minutes after the bombing for driving without a license plate. He was arrested for carrying a concealed weapon and imprisoned in a local jail. Authorities had no idea he was a bombing suspect until the FBI called on April 21, the day he was due to be released on bail. After

McVeigh was charged with the bombing, his friend Terry Nichols surrendered to police. In 1997, McVeigh was convicted of murder and conspiracy. He was executed by lethal injection on June 11, 2001, at the U.S. Penitentiary in Terre Haute, Indiana. Nichols was convicted of involuntary manslaughter and conspiracy and was sentenced to life imprisonment without parole.

Both McVeigh and Nichols were antigovernment extremists. Because the bombing took place on the second anniversary of the fire that ended the Justice Department's siege on the Branch Davidian compound at Waco, authorities believed that it was, in part, retaliation against the federal government for the deaths of the cult members. The Oklahoma City bombing was the worst terrorist attack ever perpetrated on American soil up to that time.

Search and rescue crews looked for victims trapped beneath the rubble of the Oklahoma City federal building. The remnants of the building were later demolished and cleared away, and a memorial was built on the site.

★ ★

★　★　★　★

EPILOGUE

Balancing Security and Freedom

John Ashcroft of Missouri was sworn in as America's 79th attorney general in February 2001, soon after the inauguration of President George W. Bush. No one could have imagined, however, that an event of horrific proportions would soon change the priorities of the new administration—and add a new urgency to Ashcroft's role as the chief law-enforcement officer of the United States.

On September 11, 2001, the al-Qaeda terrorist network of Islamic extremists, led by Osama bin Laden, attacked the United States by hijacking four commercial passenger jets and flying three of them into American landmarks. At about 8:48 A.M., the first jet crashed into the north tower of the World Trade Center in New York City. Minutes later, a second jetliner flew into the south tower of the Trade Center. A third jet hit the Pentagon in Washington, D.C., at about 9:43 A.M, and a fourth plane (possibly bound for the White House) crashed in a field in Pennsylvania after passengers overpowered the terrorists. By 10:30 that morning, Americans watched in shock as both towers, each 110 stories high, collapsed due to the massive fires and intense heat caused by the burning jet fuel. Close to 3,000 people died at the World Trade Center, 120 were killed at the Pentagon, and more than 250 people perished on the four jetliners.

When nominating John Ashcroft (b. 1942) as the nation's 79th attorney general, President George W. Bush called the former governor and senator "a man of great integrity, a man of great judgment, and a man who knows the law."

The destroyed World Trade Center (above) and the damaged Pentagon building after the terrorist attacks of September 11, 2001

Less than a month later, the United States military attacked al-Qaeda training camps and military installations in Afghanistan. George W. Bush announced a war against terrorists and any government that sponsored or financed them. Since the U.S. continued to receive terrorist threats, the Department of Justice and the FBI, under the direction of the attorney general, initiated the most extensive investigation in the nation's history to find, arrest, and imprison terrorists and prevent future attacks. "We have an objective . . . of saving American lives," declared John Ashcroft, "and we'll do it in the context of respecting the American Constitution and our values."

The dilemma that faced Ashcroft and the Bush administration was to find the proper balance between preserving liberty and maintaining security. In past times of war and national emergency, civil liberties have often taken a back seat to national security. This occurred during the Civil War with the suspension of habeas corpus, after World War I with the Palmer Raids, and during World War II with the internment of Japanese Americans. Critics argued that the legislative and executive orders issued in the wake of the September 11 attacks restricted civil liberties and personal freedom in a similar way. Some of the more controversial measures allowed for the indefinite detention of hundreds of non-citizens on immigration violations and permitted the questioning of thousands of males of Middle Eastern descent. They authorized the monitoring of private conversations between prisoners and their attorneys, and advocated the use of special military tribunals to try foreigners charged with terrorism (as Franklin Roosevelt did in 1942 with the eight Nazi saboteurs).

Other new measures in the war on terror included increased phone and Internet surveillance by law-enforcement agencies, searches of individual homes, and expanded government access to medical, financial, and education records. The attorney general was also empowered to designate certain domestic groups as terrorist organizations and deport any non-citizens who belonged to them. The FBI's authority was expanded to monitor political groups and religious organizations if they were suspected of supporting or engaging in acts of terror. Further new regulations by Ashcroft included fingerprinting and photographing of all foreign students, tourists, and visitors upon entering the country, and requiring registration with the Immigration and Naturalization Service (INS) after 30 days. President Bush also created a new agency called the Department of Homeland Security, to be headed by a cabinet-level secretary. Two agencies that were previously part of the Justice Department—the INS and the Office of Domestic Preparedness—were moved to the new department.

Most Americans supported the measures taken by the president and the attorney general. Some supporters noted that America's strong commitment to personal liberty had aided the terrorists in the first place, by allowing them to enter the country, move around freely, and even take flying lessons. Opponents warned, however, that the new measures were dangerous and that once certain freedoms were taken away, it would be hard to get them back again. There were widespread complaints about racial profiling, namely the targeting of Arab males as prime terrorist suspects. The American Muslim community was placed under increased scrutiny, since all of the 19 hijackers had been Islamic extremists of Middle Eastern descent. Arab Americans, the vast majority of whom were peaceful and law-abiding citizens, expressed concern about being the primary focus of the Justice Department's investigations.

Throughout American history, whenever civil liberties were restricted or personal freedom threatened, it was public outcry that eventually held such excesses in check. As the feeling of safety and security returned, the balance reasserted itself and people favored more political and personal freedom. This may happen in the case of terrorism. If the threat of domestic terrorism increases in the future,

racial profiling: a set of characteristics or qualities based on race or ethnic background that authorities use in attempting to identify possible criminal suspects however, the public might demand that the attorney general use the full power and reach of the U.S. government to hunt down and punish terrorists. How far the Constitution would allow the government to go in the interest of promoting domestic security would be left for the courts to decide. Nonetheless, the outlook for the future favors a more active and high-profile role for the attorney general in the federal government. This is in keeping with the historical expansion of the duties and responsibilities of the office. As the chief law-enforcement officer of the executive branch, the attorney general will, among other tasks, oversee and coordinate intelligence-gathering agencies within the United States and bring to justice those who pose a threat to the security of the nation.

President George W. Bush with Alberto Gonzales, who on February 3, 2005, was sworn in as the nation's 80th attorney general, the first Hispanic American ever to hold the office. Gonzales told Department of Justice employees that they have "a special obligation to protect America against future acts of terrorism."

ATTORNEYS GENERAL

	date of appointment	president(s) served
Edmund Randolph	September 26, 1789	Washington
William Bradford	January 27, 1794	Washington
Charles Lee	December 10, 1795	Washington, J. Adams
Levi Lincoln	March 5, 1801	Jefferson
John Breckenridge	August 7, 1805	Jefferson
Caesar A. Rodney	January 20, 1807	Jefferson, Madison
William Pinkney	December 11, 1811	Madison
Richard Rush	February 10, 1814	Madison, Monroe
William Wirt	November 13, 1817	Monroe, J. Q. Adams
John M. Berrien	March 9, 1829	Jackson
Roger B. Taney	July 20, 1831	Jackson
Benjamin F. Butler	November 15, 1833	Jackson, Van Buren
Felix Grundy	July 5, 1838	Van Buren
Henry D. Gilpin	January 11, 1840	Van Buren
John J. Crittenden*	March 5, 1841	W. H. Harrison, Tyler
Hugh S. Legare	September 13, 1841	Tyler
John Nelson	July 1, 1843	Tyler
John Y. Mason	March 6, 1845	Polk
Nathan Clifford	October 17, 1846	Polk
Isaac Toucey	June 21, 1848	Polk
Reverdy Johnson	March 8, 1849	Taylor
John J. Crittenden*	July 22, 1850	Fillmore
Caleb Cushing	March 7, 1853	Pierce
Jeremiah S. Black	March 6, 1857	Buchanan
Edwin M. Stanton	December 20, 1860	Buchanan
Edward Bates	March 5, 1861	Lincoln
James Speed	December 2, 1864	Lincoln, A. Johnson
Henry Stanbery	July 23, 1866	A. Johnson
William M. Evarts	July 15, 1868	A. Johnson
Ebenezer R. Hoar	March 5, 1869	Grant
Amos T. Akerman	June 23, 1870	Grant
George H. Williams	December 14, 1871	Grant
Edwards Pierrepont	April 26, 1875	Grant
Alphonso Taft	May 22, 1876	Grant
Charles Devens	March 12, 1877	Hayes
Wayne MacVeagh	March 5, 1881	Garfield
Benjamin H. Brewster	December 19, 1882	Arthur

*served in the same position twice

Augustus H. Garland	March 6, 1885	Cleveland
William H. H. Miller	March 5, 1889	B. Harrison
Richard Olney	March 6, 1893	Cleveland
Judson Harmon	June 8, 1895	Cleveland
Joseph McKenna	March 5, 1897	McKinley
John W. Griggs	June 25, 1898	McKinley
Philander C. Knox	April 5, 1901	McKinley, T. Roosevelt
William H. Moody	July 1, 1904	T. Roosevelt
Charles J. Bonaparte	December 17, 1906	T. Roosevelt
George W. Wickersham	March 5, 1909	Taft
James C. McReynolds	March 5, 1913	Wilson
Thomas W. Gregory	August 29, 1914	Wilson
A. Mitchell Palmer	March 5, 1919	Wilson
Harry M. Daugherty	March 4, 1921	Harding, Coolidge
Harlan F. Stone	April 7, 1924	Coolidge
John G. Sargent	March 17, 1925	Coolidge
William D. Mitchell	March 5, 1929	Hoover
Homer S. Cummings	March 4, 1933	F. D. Roosevelt
Frank Murphy	January 2, 1939	F. D. Roosevelt
Robert H. Jackson	January 18, 1940	F. D. Roosevelt
Francis Biddle	September 5, 1941	F. D. Roosevelt
Thomas C. Clark	June 15, 1945	Truman
J. Howard McGrath	August 24, 1949	Truman
James P. McGranery	May 27, 1952	Truman
Herbert Brownell Jr.	January 21, 1953	Eisenhower
William P. Rogers	November 8, 1957	Eisenhower
Robert F. Kennedy	January 21, 1961	Kennedy, L. B. Johnson
Nicholas Katzenbach	September 4, 1964	L. B. Johnson
Ramsey Clark	March 3, 1967	L. B. Johnson
John N. Mitchell	January 21, 1969	Nixon
Richard G. Kleindienst	June 12, 1972	Nixon
Elliot Richardson	May 25, 1973	Nixon
William B. Saxbe	January 4, 1974	Nixon, Ford
Edward H. Levi	February 7, 1975	Ford
Griffin B. Bell	January 26, 1977	Carter
Benjamin R. Civiletti	August 16, 1979	Carter
William French Smith	January 23, 1981	Reagan
Edwin Meese III	February 23, 1985	Reagan
Richard Thornburgh	August 12, 1988	Reagan, G. H. W. Bush
William P. Barr	November 26, 1991	G. H. W. Bush
Janet Reno	March 12, 1993	Clinton
John Ashcroft	February 1, 2001	G. W. Bush
Alberto R. Gonzales	February 3, 2005	G. W. Bush

GLOSSARY

acquit: to free or clear someone of a legal charge or accusation

affirmative action: governmental efforts to improve the job or educational opportunities of minority groups and women

amicus curiae: an interested person or government official who may participate in a lawsuit between other parties without becoming a party. Often used in civil rights cases, it allows the government to expand its role and develop new policies.

amnesty: a pardon for past offenses

anarchist: an opponent of all forms of political authority

appeal: a request made after a trial, asking a higher court (usually a court of appeals) to reverse or set aside the decision made at the trial level

appropriation: money authorized for a specific purpose

bail: property or money given to obtain a release from legal custody

binding precedent: a legal decision that must be followed, and serves as a rule for similar cases that come later

brief: a written statement submitted by a lawyer before a case is argued in court. The brief contains all the facts, evidence, and legal issues related to the case, and explains to the judges how they should decide and why.

cabinet: a group of presidential advisors that mainly consists of the heads of the executive departments of the federal government. Cabinet members are nominated by the president, but they must be confirmed by the Senate.

censure: an official reprimand

circumstantial: not direct; secondary or incidental. Under the law, any evidence that is not eyewitness testimony is circumstantial.

clemency: an act of mercy or forgiveness; willingness to lessen the severity of a punishment

communist: a supporter of a theoretical political and economic system based on government ownership of property

conflict of interest: a clash between personal interests and official responsibilities of a person in an official position of trust

conservative: one who generally believes in limiting, rather than expanding, the role of government in society

conviction: a judgment by a jury or judge that a person is guilty of a crime as charged

counsel: a lawyer giving legal advice or conducting a case in court

desegregation: the elimination of restrictions separating the races in public facilities

disenfranchise: to deprive a person of the right to vote

espionage: the use of spies by governments, corporations, or organizations to discover military, political, technical, or personal secrets

extradition: the surrender of someone charged with a crime for trial by one state or country to another

impeachment: formal charges of misconduct against a public official

incumbent: a person currently holding an office

independent counsel (sometimes called **independent prosecutor**): a nonpartisan attorney approved by representatives of both major parties to conduct a thorough investigation of a particular event or individual

indictment: a formal statement that charges a person with a crime

internment: the confinement, especially during wartime, of a group of people

judicial review: examination of a government official or entity's actions by a court of law

jurisdiction: the authority to administer justice in a particular area

liberalism: a set of political or social beliefs that emphasizes reform, progress, tolerance, and protection of civil liberties through the actions of government

litigation: engagement in legal proceedings; a lawsuit

misdemeanor: a criminal offense less serious than a felony

naturalize: to grant full citizenship to someone of foreign birth

opinion: an attorney general's formal answer to a specific legal question asked by a public official; also, a judge's written statement announcing a court's decision and giving the reasons for it. An opinion by a court is legally binding, while an opinion by an attorney general is merely advisory, though it can carry weight in court.

pending: not yet decided; awaiting a trial or settlement

precedent: a legal decision that serves as an example or justification when deciding a later case

pro bono: legal work done by lawyers free of charge

prosecution: legal action initiated against a person; also, the lawyer or lawyers empowered to conduct such action on behalf of a government and its people

racial profiling: a set of characteristics or qualities based on race or ethnic background that authorities use in attempting to identify possible criminal suspects

saboteur: a person who commits sabotage, the deliberate damage of equipment or property to undermine a government or military operation

socialist: a supporter of a political system in which the means of producing and distributing goods and services is either owned collectively or owned by a government that plans and controls the economy

suffrage: the right to vote

tenure: the period or term of holding an office

U.S. attorney: the lawyer in charge of prosecuting federal crimes within a certain judicial district of the United States, appointed by the president

warrant: a document authorizing an official to perform a specific act, such as ordering a payment of funds, conducting a search, or performing an arrest

writ of habeas corpus: a court order directed to authorities who have a person in custody to bring the prisoner before a judge or court and show cause as to why that person has been arrested or detained

SOURCE NOTES

Quoted passages are noted by page and order of citation.

Introduction

p. 7: Nancy V. Baker, *Conflicting Loyalties: Law and Politics in the Attorney General's Office, 1789-1990* (Wichita: University Press of Kansas, 1992), 51.

pp. 7-8: Baker, *Conflicting Loyalties*, 48.

p. 9 (margin): Baker, *Conflicting Loyalties*, 53.

p. 10: Luther A. Huston, Arthur Selwyn Miller, Samuel Krislov, and Robert G. Dixon Jr., *Roles of the Attorney General of the United States* (Washington: American Enterprise Institute, 1968), 5.

Chapter One: William Wirt

p. 15 (first): John P. Kennedy, *Memoirs of the Life of William Wirt, Attorney General of the United States*, Volume 1 (Philadelphia: Lea and Blanchard, 1849), 408.

p. 15 (second): Kennedy, *Memoirs*, Volume 1, 413.

p. 15 (third): Kennedy, *Memoirs*, Volume 2, 44.

p. 15 (fourth): Kennedy, *Memoirs*, Volume 2, 67.

pp. 20-21: Kennedy, *Memoirs*, Volume 2, 16.

p. 22 (first margin): Huston, et. al., *Roles of the Attorney General*, 19-20.

p. 22 (second margin): Baker, *Conflicting Loyalties*, 57.

p. 23: Baker, *Conflicting Loyalties*, 16.

p. 24 (caption): Dartmouth College, "A Brief History," www.dartmouth.edu/about/history.html.

p. 24 (first): Huston, et. al., *Roles of the Attorney General*, 28.

p. 24 (second): Huston, et. al., *Roles of the Attorney General*, 28.

p. 26: Baker, *Conflicting Loyalties*, 127.

Chapter Two: Edward Bates

p. 32 (margin): Marvin R. Cain, *Lincoln's Attorney General Edward Bates of Missouri* (Columbia: University of Missouri Press, 1965), 64.

p. 37 (first margin): William H. Rehnquist, *All the Laws But One: Civil Liberties in Wartime* (New York: Knopf, 1998), 36.

p. 37 (second margin): Rehnquist, *All the Laws But One*, ii.

p. 37: Rehnquist, *All the Laws But One*, 25.

p. 38 (first): H. Jefferson Powell, *The Constitution and the Attorneys General* (Durham, N.C.: Carolina Academic Press, 1999), 172.

p. 38 (second): Powell, *The Constitution*, 173.

p. 40 (margin): Homer Cummings and Carl McFarland, *Federal Justice: Chapters in the History of Justice and the Federal Executive* (New York: Macmillan, 1937), 204.

p. 40: Cain, *Lincoln's Attorney General*, 230.

pp. 41-42: Powell, *The Constitution*, 196.

p. 43 (caption): Huston, et. al., *Roles of the Attorney General*, 19.

p. 43: Howard K. Beale, ed., *The Diary of Edward Bates 1859-1866* (Washington: U.S. Government Printing Office, 1933), 483.

Chapter Three: A. Mitchell Palmer

p. 45: Edwin P. Hoyt, *The Palmer Raids, 1919-1920: An Attempt to Suppress Dissent* (New York: Seabury, 1969), 31.

p. 48 (margin): Stanley Coben, *A. Mitchell Palmer: Politician* (New York: Da Capo, 1972), 71.

p. 51 (first): Robert K. Murray, *Red Scare: A Study in National Hysteria, 1919-1920* (Minneapolis: University of Minnesota, 1955), 78.

p. 51 (second): Murray, *Red Scare*, 71.

p. 51 (third): Coben, *A. Mitchell Palmer*, 205.

p. 53: Coben, *A. Mitchell Palmer*, 215.

p. 54 (first): Roberta Strauss Feuerlicht, *America's Reign of Terror: World War I, the Red Scare, and the Palmer Raids* (New York: Random House, 1971), 79.

p. 54 (second): Coben, *A. Mitchell Palmer,* 196.

p. 56: Murray, *Red Scare*, 208.

p. 57 (first margin): Murray, *Red Scare*, 248.

p. 57 (second margin): Hoyt, *The Palmer Raids*, 55.

p. 59: Coben, *A. Mitchell Palmer*, 266.

Chapter Four: Francis Biddle

p. 61: Francis Biddle, *In Brief Authority* (Garden City, N.Y.: Doubleday, 1962), 4.

pp. 61-62: Biddle, *In Brief Authority*, 7.

p. 63: Alden Whitman, "Francis Biddle is Dead at 82; Roosevelt's Attorney General," *New York Times*, October 5, 1968.

p. 65 (margin): Biddle, *In Brief Authority*, 108.

p. 67 (first): Biddle, *In Brief Authority*, 185.

p. 67 (second): Biddle, *In Brief Authority*, 207.

p. 69 (margin): Biddle, *In Brief Authority*, 212.

p. 69 (first): Biddle, *In Brief Authority*, 213.

p. 69 (second): Biddle, *In Brief Authority*, 218.

p. 69 (third): Biddle, *In Brief Authority*, 219.

p. 72 (first): Rehnquist, *All the Laws But One*, 195.

p. 72 (second): Rehnquist, *All the Laws But One*, 199.

p. 72 (third): Rehnquist, *All the Laws But One*, 200-201.

p. 73: Greg Robinson, *By Order of the President: FDR and the Internment of Japanese Americans* (Cambridge, Mass.: Harvard University Press, 2001), 251.

p. 74: Michi Nishiura Weglyn, *Years of Infamy: The Untold Story of America's Concentration Camps* (Seattle: University of Washington Press, 1996), 314.

p. 75: Biddle, *In Brief Authority*, 332.

p. 76 (first): Biddle, *In Brief Authority*, 338.

p. 76 (second): Biddle, *In Brief Authority*, 340.

p. 76 (third): Biddle, *In Brief Authority*, 339.

p. 78 (first): Biddle, *In Brief Authority*, 483.

p. 78 (second): Biddle, *In Brief Authority*, 226.

Chapter Five: Herbert Brownell

p. 81 (first): Herbert Brownell, *Advising Ike* (Lawrence: University Press of Kansas, 1993), 1.

p. 81 (second): Brownell, *Advising Ike*, 2.

p. 83: Brownell, *Advising Ike*, 23.

p. 85: Brownell, *Advising Ike*, 132.

p. 87 (first): "Constitution of the United States," *The World Almanac and Book of Facts* (New York: World Almanac Books, 2002), 535.

p. 87 (second): Donald B. King and Charles W. Quick, eds., *Legal Aspects of the Civil Rights Movement* (Detroit: Wayne State University Press, 1965), 13.

p. 88 (first): Brownell, *Advising Ike*, 193.

p. 88 (second): Brownell, *Advising Ike*, 189.

p. 88 (third): Richard Kluger, *Simple Justice: The History of* Brown v. Board of Education *and Black America's Struggle for Equality*, Volume 2 (New York: Knopf, 1975), 890.

p. 89: Brownell, *Advising Ike*, 197.

p. 91: Brownell, *Advising Ike*, 375.

p. 92 (margin): Brownell, *Advising Ike*, 221.

p. 92 (first): Brownell, *Advising Ike*, 213.

p. 92 (second): Brownell, *Advising Ike*, 218.

p. 92 (third): Brownell, *Advising Ike*, 219.

pp. 92-93: Brownell, *Advising Ike*, 220.

p. 94 (first): Kluger, *Simple Justice*, 951.

p. 94 (second, third, and fourth): Brownell, *Advising Ike*, 215.

p. 95 (first): Cornell W. Clayton, *The Politics of Justice: The Attorney General and the Making of Legal Policy* (Armonk, N.Y.: Sharpe, 1992), 133.

p. 95 (second): Brownell, *Advising Ike*, 187.

p. 95 (third): Brownell, *Advising Ike*, 302.

Chapter Six: Robert F. Kennedy

p. 98 (first): Arthur M. Schlesinger Jr., *Robert Kennedy and His Times* (Boston: Houghton Mifflin, 1978), 874.

p. 98 (second): Evan Thomas, *Robert Kennedy: His Life* (New York: Simon and Schuster, 2000), 366.

pp. 98-99: Schlesinger, *Robert Kennedy*, 874-875.

p. 99: Schlesinger, *Robert Kennedy*, 286.

p. 100 (margin): Schlesinger, *Robert Kennedy*, 81.

p. 103 (margin): Schlesinger, *Robert Kennedy*, 218.

p. 106 (caption): Schlesinger, *Robert Kennedy*, 325.

p. 106: Robert F. Kennedy, *Robert Kennedy in His Own Words: The Unpublished Recollections of the Kennedy Years* (New York: Bantam, 1988), 165.

p. 107: Schlesinger, *Robert Kennedy*, 337.

p. 108: Kluger, *Simple Justice*, Volume 2, 954-955.

p. 109: Robert F. Kennedy, *The Pursuit of Justice* (New York: Harper & Row, 1964), 82.

p. 112: Harris Wofford, *Of Kennedys and Kings: Making Sense of the Sixties* (Pittsburgh: University of Pittsburgh Press, 1980), 419.

Chapter Seven: Edwin Meese III

p. 117 (first): Sanford J. Ungar, "Ed the Ordinary," *Esquire*, July 1986.

p. 117 (second): Ungar, "Ed the Ordinary."

p. 121 (first): Clayton, *The Politics of Justice*, 6.

p. 121 (second): Jacob V. Lamar, "The Crusading Attorney General: Edwin Meese Tilts at the Courts, Quotas, and Criminal Rights," *Time*, September 9, 1985.

p. 122: Clayton, *The Politics of Justice*, 140.

p. 124 (margin): Baker, *Conflicting Loyalties*, 97.

p. 124 (first): Edwin Meese III, *With Reagan: The Inside Story* (Washington: Regnery Gateway, 1992), 313.

p. 124 (second): Ezra Bowen, "Judges with Their Minds Right: The President Pushes for Conservative Control of the Bench," *Time*, November 4, 1985.

p. 124 (third): Douglas W. Kmiec, *The Attorney General's Lawyer: Inside the Meese Justice Department* (New York: Praeger, 1992), 18.

p. 124 (fourth and fifth): Bowen, "Judges with Their Minds Right."

p. 124 (sixth): Clayton, *The Politics of Justice*, 157.

p. 124 (seventh): Ezra Bowen, "Radical in Conservative Garb," *Time*, August 11, 1986.

p. 124 (eighth): Lamar, "The Crusading Attorney General."

p. 125 (first): Richard Lacayo, "Supreme or Not Supreme: That Is the Question, Says the Attorney General," *Time*, November 3, 1986.

p. 125 (second): Lacayo, "Supreme or Not Supreme."

p. 126 (first): Meese, *With Reagan*, 318.

p. 126 (second): "Adieu," *The Economist,* July 9, 1988.

Chapter Eight: Janet Reno

p. 131: Paul Anderson, *Janet Reno: Doing the Right Thing* (New York: John Wiley, 1994), 38.

p. 132 (first margin): Anderson, *Janet Reno*, 21.

p. 132 (second margin): Anderson, *Janet Reno*, 34.

p. 132 (first): Anderson, *Janet Reno*, 40.

p. 132 (second): Anderson, *Janet Reno*, 12.

pp. 132-133: Anderson, *Janet Reno*, 42.

p. 137 (first): "Attorney General Janet Reno's Opening Statement Before the Crime Subcommittee of the House Judiciary Committee and the National Security International Affairs and Criminal Justice Subcommittee of the House Government Reforms and Oversight Committee," August 1, 1995, www.pbs.org/wgbh/pages/frontline/waco/renoopeningst.html.

p. 137 (second): Nancy Gibbs, "Oh My God, They're Killing Themselves!" *Time*, May 3, 1993.

p. 138: Gibbs, "Oh My God," 1993.

p. 139 (first): Anderson, *Janet Reno*, 195.

p. 139 (second): Anderson, *Janet Reno*, 42.

p. 140: Susan Schmidt, "Investigation Clears Agents at Waco," *Washington Post*, July 22, 2000.

p. 144 (first): David A. Vise, "Reno Recalls Successes, Difficulties in Farewell: Attorney General Plans Cross-Country Drive," *Washington Post*, January 12, 2001.

p. 144 (second): Helen Kim, "Stanford U. Interview: Reno Reflects on Policy, Life," *The America's Intelligence Wire*, April 9, 2003.

p. 145: David A. Vise, "For Reno, Connections Made Outside Beltway: Greatest Support Came Away from Washington," *Washington Post*, January 22, 2001.

Epilogue

p. 149 (caption): U.S. Department of Justice, "Attorney General John Ashcroft," www.usdoj.gov/ag/ashcroftbio.html.

p. 151: "An 'Unapologetic' Ashcroft: Tough and Unrepentant, the Attorney General Defends the Nationwide Dragnet, and Puts Terrorists on Notice," *Newsweek*, December 10, 2001.

p. 153: "Attorney General Alberto Gonzales," www.whitehouse.gov/government/gonzales-bio.html.

BIBLIOGRAPHY

"Adieu." *The Economist*, July 9, 1988.

Anderson, J. W. *Eisenhower, Brownell, and the Congress: The Tangled Origins of the Civil Rights Bill of 1956-1957*. University, Ala.: University of Alabama Press, 1964.

Anderson, Paul. *Janet Reno: Doing the Right Thing*. New York: John Wiley, 1994.

Associated Press. "Reno Says Show—But Not Use—Of Force Was Necessary." www.courttv.com/archive/national/2000/0427/elian-reno_ap.html.

"Attorney General Janet Reno's Opening Statement Before the Crime Subcommittee of the House Judiciary Committee and the National Security International Affairs and Criminal Justice Subcommittee of the House Government Reforms and Oversight Committee," August 1, 1995, www.pbs.org/wgbh/pages/frontline/waco/renoopeningst.html.

Attorneys General of the United States: 1789-1985. Washington: United States Department of Justice, 1985.

Baker, Nancy V. *Conflicting Loyalties: Law and Politics in the Attorney General's Office, 1789-1990*. Wichita: University Press of Kansas, 1992.

Beale, Howard K., ed. *The Diary of Edward Bates: 1859-1866*. Washington: U.S. Government Printing Office, 1933.

Biddle, Francis. *A Casual Past*. Garden City, N.Y.: Doubleday, 1961.

———. *In Brief Authority*. Garden City, N.Y.: Doubleday, 1962.

Bowen, Ezra. "Judges with Their Minds Right: The President Pushes for Conservative Control of the Bench." *Time*, November 4, 1985.

———. "Radical in Conservative Garb." *Time*, August 11, 1986.

Brownell, Herbert. *Advising Ike*. Lawrence: University Press of Kansas, 1993.

Cain, Marvin R. *Lincoln's Attorney General Edward Bates of Missouri*. Columbia: University of Missouri Press, 1965.

Clayton, Cornell W. *The Politics of Justice: The Attorney General and the Making of Legal Policy*. Armonk, N.Y.: Sharpe, 1992.

Coben, Stanley. *A. Mitchell Palmer: Politician*. New York: Da Capo, 1972.

Cohen, Adam. "Rough Justice: The Attorney General Has Powerful New Tools to Fight Terrorism. Has He Gone Too Far?" *Time*, December 10, 2001.

Cummings, Homer, and Carl McFarland. *Federal Justice: Chapters in the History of Justice and the Federal Executive*. New York: Macmillan, 1937.

"The Days Dwindle Down for Edwin Meese." *U.S. News & World Report*, April 11, 1988.

Emert, Phyllis Raybin. *World War II: On the Homefront*. Carlisle, Mass.: Discovery Enterprises, 1996.

Fairclough, Adam. *Better Day Coming: Blacks and Equality, 1890-2000*. New York: Viking, 2001.

Feuerlicht, Roberta Strauss. *America's Reign of Terror: World War I, the Red Scare, and the Palmer Raids*. New York: Random House, 1971.

Garraty, John A., and Mark C. Carnes, eds. *American National Biography*. New York: Oxford University Press, 1999.

Gibbs, Nancy. "Oh My God, They're Killing Themselves!" *Time*, May 3, 1993.

Greider, William. "Give Meese a Chance and the Federal Courts Will Be Singing Reagan's Far-Right Song." *Rolling Stone*, June 6, 1985.

Hoyt, Edwin P. *The Palmer Raids, 1919-1920: An Attempt to Suppress Dissent*. New York: Seabury, 1969.

Huston, Luther A. *The Department of Justice*. New York: Praeger, 1967.

Huston, Luther A., Arthur Selwyn Miller, Samuel Krislov, and Robert G. Dixon Jr. *Roles of the Attorney General of the United States*. Washington: American Enterprise Institute, 1968.

Kennedy, John P. *Memoirs of the Life of William Wirt, Attorney General of the United States*. 2 vols. Philadelphia: Lea and Blanchard, 1849.

Kennedy, Robert F. *The Pursuit of Justice*. New York: Harper & Row, 1964.

———. *Robert Kennedy in His Own Words: The Unpublished Recollections of the Kennedy Years*. New York: Bantam, 1988.

Kim, Helen. "Stanford U. Interview: Reno Reflects on Policy, Life." *The America's Intelligence Wire*, April 9, 2003.

King, Donald B., and Charles W. Quick, eds. *Legal Aspects of the Civil Rights Movement*. Detroit: Wayne State University Press, 1965.

Kluger, Richard. *Simple Justice: The History of* Brown v. Board of Education *and Black America's Struggle for Equality*. 2 vols. New York: Knopf, 1975.

Kmiec, Douglas W. *The Attorney General's Lawyer: Inside the Meese Justice Department*. New York: Praeger, 1992.

Lacayo, Richard. "Supreme or Not Supreme: That Is the Question, Says the Attorney General." *Time*, November 3, 1986.

Lamar, Jacob V. "The Crusading Attorney General: Edwin Meese Tilts at the Courts, Quotas, and Criminal Rights." *Time*, September 9, 1985.

Meese, Edwin III. *With Reagan: The Inside Story*. Washington: Regnery Gateway, 1992.

Murray, Robert K. *Red Scare: A Study in National Hysteria, 1919-1920*. Minneapolis: University of Minnesota, 1955.

Powell, H. Jefferson. *The Constitution and the Attorneys General*. Durham, N.C.: Carolina Academic Press, 1999.

Rehnquist, William H. *All the Laws But One: Civil Liberties in Wartime*. New York: Knopf, 1998.

Robinson, Greg. *By Order of the President: FDR and the Internment of Japanese Americans*. Cambridge, Mass.: Harvard University Press, 2001.

Schlesinger, Arthur M., Jr. *Robert Kennedy and His Times*. Boston: Houghton Mifflin, 1978.

Schmidt, Susan. "Investigation Clears Agents at Waco." *Washington Post*, July 22, 2000.

Steel, Ronald. *In Love with Night: The American Romance with Robert Kennedy*. New York: Simon and Schuster, 2000.

Thomas, Evan. *Robert Kennedy: His Life*. New York: Simon and Schuster, 2000.

"An 'Unapologetic' Ashcroft: Tough and Unrepentant, the Attorney General Defends the Nationwide Dragnet, and Puts Terrorists on Notice." *Newsweek*, December 10, 2001.

Ungar, Sanford J. "Ed the Ordinary." *Esquire*, July 1986.

Vise, David A. "For Reno, Connections Made Outside Beltway: Greatest Support Came Away from Washington." *Washington Post*, January 22, 2001.

———. "Reno Recalls Successes, Difficulties in Farewell: Attorney General Plans Cross-Country Drive." *Washington Post*, January 12, 2001.

Vise, David A., and Lorraine Adams. "Revelations Inflame Rift Between Justice Department and FBI: Waco Controversy and Hill Inquiries Expose Differences." *Washington Post*, September 27, 1999.

Weglyn, Michi Nishiura. *Years of Infamy: The Untold Story of America's Concentration Camps*. Seattle: University of Washington Press, 1996.

Whitman, Alden. "Francis Biddle Is Dead at 82; Roosevelt's Attorney General." *New York Times*, October 5, 1968.

Wofford, Harris. *Of Kennedys and Kings: Making Sense of the Sixties*. Pittsburgh: University of Pittsburgh Press, 1980.

INDEX

Adams, John, 15

Adams, John Quincy, 25, 26

affirmative action, 125

al-Qaeda, 149, 151

Alabama, University of, 107

Alcohol, Tobacco, and Firearms, Bureau of (ATF), 136

Alexander v. Holmes, 122

Alfred P. Murrah Federal Building, 146

Alien Land Act, 69

aliens, enemy, 64-65, 67, 69

American Civil Liberties Union, 125

American Legion, 54

American Party, 29, 34. *See also* "Know-Nothings"

Americans for Democratic Action, 78

amicus curiae, 88, 124

anarchists, 45-46, 50, 54, 56

Anti-Masonic Party, 26

Antitrust Division (DOJ), 13

antiwar protests, 117, 119

Ashcroft, John, 13, 149, 151, 152

Baird, Zoë, 135-136

Baker, James, 120

Baltimore, Union troops attacked in, 36, 37

Barnett, Ross, 105

Bates, Caroline (mother), 31

Bates, Edward: appointed attorney general, 34; death of, 43; early years of, 30-31; as lawyer, 31, 32; as leader in Whig Party, 32, 33-34; as member of American Party (Know-Nothings), 33-34; in Missouri legislature, 31, 32; opposition of, to military power over civilians, 38, 40, 43; resignation of, 42; responsibilities of, as attorney general, 39-40; support of, for suspension of habeas corpus, 13, 38, 43

Bates, Fleming (son), 40

Bates, Frederick (brother), 31-32

Bates, John (son), 40

Bates, Julia Coalter (wife), 31

Bates, Thomas (father), 30, 31

Berkeley, University of California at, 115-116, 118, 119

Berrien, John, 10, 11

Bethel School District v. Fraser, 124

Biden, Joseph, 136

Biddle, Algernon Sydney (father), 62

Biddle, Frances (mother), 62

Biddle, Francis: appointed attorney general, 65; death of, 79; early years of, 61, 62; as judge in Nuremberg trials, 77-78; as lawyer, 62, 63; as member of Progressive Party, 62-63; opposition of, to internment of Japanese Americans, 13, 62, 69, 74, 78, 79; positions of, in Roosevelt administration, 63-64; relationship of, with Roosevelt, 61-62, 63, 69, 74; as solicitor general, 64

Biddle, Katherine Garrison Chapin (wife), 63

Black, Hugo, 72, 73

Blackmun, Harry, 123

Black Panthers, 97

Blair, Montgomery, 35

Blannerhassett, Harman, 19

Bolsheviks, 50, 51, 54

Bowron, Fletcher, 68

Brady, James, 120

Branch Davidians, 136, 137, 138, 139, 140, 147

Brennan, William, 124

Broadnax, Lydia, 18-19

Brown, Ernest, 131-132

Brown, Linda, 86, 88

Brown, Michael, 18

Brown, Pat, 116

Brownell, Doris McCarter (wife), 83, 85

Brownell, Herbert: appointed attorney general, 82, 85; civil rights legislation proposed by, 13, 92-94, 95; death of, 95; early years of, 82; as Eisenhower's campaign manager, 85; as lawyer, 81, 82-83, 85, 94-95; as leader in Republican Party, 83-85; support of, for desegregation, 81, 82, 88, 91

Brownell, May (mother), 82

Brownell, Samuel (brother), 81

Brownell, Herbert, Sr. (father), 82

Brown v. Board of Education, 82, 85-86, 88, 89, 90, 94; *Brown II*, 88, 89

Buchanan, James, 34

Buford, 56

Bunche, Ralph, 100

Burger, Warren, 122, 126

Burr, Aaron, 19, 20, 26

Bush, George W., 149, 151, 152, 153

Bush, Jeb, 142-143

cabinet, 8, 13, 22, 26, 32, 62, 81, 94; of Franklin Roosevelt, 61, 66, 67; of Kennedy, 103, 107; of Lincoln, 34, 35, 42; of Reagan, 120, 129; of Washington, 9, 61; of Wilson, 48, 49

Cadwalader, George, 37

California, Japanese Americans in, 67-68, 69, 70

Cameron, Simon, 35

Carr, Dabney, 20

Carswell, Harold, 122-123

Carter, Jimmy, 119, 123

Center for Criminal Justice Policy and Management, 119

Chase, Salmon P., 35, 42

Cherokee Indians, 26

Chiang Kai-Shek (Madame), 61

circuit courts of appeal, 8

civil rights, 13, 81, 94, 95, 103; during Civil War, 30, 39, 40, 43; of Japanese Americans during WWII, 61, 62, 67-68, 69-71, 72-74, 79; legislation protecting, 82, 92-94, 108, 109, 113; Palmer's violations of, 55-57, 58, 59; restricted after September 11, 151-153; Supreme Court cases affecting, 41, 82, 85, 86-89, 103, 105, 109, 122

Civil Rights Act of 1957, 93, 94

Civil Rights Act of 1964, 108, 109, 110

Civil Rights Division (DOJ), 13

civil rights movement, 85, 97, 103, 107, 115

Civil War, 12, 13, 27, 29, 34, 82; aftermath of, 42-43, 87; habeas

corpus suspended during, 37-39, 151

Clinton, Bill, 135-136, 138, 139, 140, 141, 142, 144

Coben, Stanley, 59

Cold War, 103

Commission on Wartime Relocation and Internment of Civilians (CWRIC), 73

Communist Party, 50

communists, 46, 50, 56, 78

Confederate States of America, 34, 35, 38, 39, 40, 42, 87

Confiscation Act, Second, 41

Confiscation Bill, 40

Congress, U.S., 8, 22-23, 51, 57, 66, 75; acts and bills passed by, 38, 39, 40, 42, 93, 94, 108; position of attorney general defined by, 10, 11, 27; powers of, 24, 25, 38

Conspiracies Act, 40

Constitution, U.S., 24, 37, 38, 41, 72, 88, 92, 109, 151, 153; amendments to, 87, 88, 94, 124; interpretation of, 124

Coolidge, Calvin, 81

Court of Appeals, U.S., 123

Court of International Trade, 8

Criminal Division (DOJ), 100

Cushing, Caleb, 11, 12, 27

ABOUT THE AUTHOR

Phyllis Raybin Emert is the author of more than 40 books on a wide variety of subjects. She received a B.A. degree in political science from the State University of New York at Stony Brook, focusing on American history and politics. Emert received her M.A. degree from Penn State in political science and public administration. She lives in northern New Jersey with her husband, Larry, and has two grown children, Melissa and Matt.

PHOTO CREDITS